WRITING EFFECTIVE COURSE ASSIGNMENTS

WRITING EFFECTIVE COURSE ASSIGNMENTS

A Guide to Non-Degree and
Undergraduate Students

Elia Shabani Mligo

RESOURCE *Publications* • Eugene, Oregon

WRITING EFFECTIVE COURSE ASSIGNMENTS
A Guide to Non-Degree and Undergraduate Students

Copyright © 2017 Elia Shabani Mligo. All rights reserved. Except for brief quotations in critical publications or reviews, no part of this book may be reproduced in any manner without prior written permission from the publisher. Write: Permissions, Wipf and Stock Publishers, 199 W. 8th Ave., Suite 3, Eugene, OR 97401.

Resource Publications
An Imprint of Wipf and Stock Publishers
199 W. 8th Ave., Suite 3
Eugene, OR 97401

www.wipfandstock.com

PAPERBACK ISBN: 978-1-5326-1698-3
HARDCOVER ISBN: 978-1-4982-4133-5
EBOOK ISBN: 978-1-4982-4132-8

Manufactured in the U.S.A.   MAY 10, 2017

To Non-Degree and Undergraduate Students in Colleges and Universities for their efforts to survive the adversity of academic writing; this book is your release!

CONTENTS

Acknowledgments | ix

1 Introduction | 1

2 Writing Your Assignment | 6

3 Documenting Sources in Your Assignment | 47

4 Using Sources in Writing Your Assignment | 79

5 Organizing Ideas in Your Assignment | 94

6 Constructing Informed Argument | 110

7 Conclusion | 152

Bibliography | 155

ACKNOWLEDGMENTS

IT IS HARDLY POSSIBLE to develop a massive and constructive idea from just a single head. This assertion has been the reality in my development of this book. The idea began with me; however, the development of the idea has been a shared endeavor. I owe thanks to the contributions of many people towards the present form of this book. The following are worth mentioning: colleagues at theUniversity of Iringa, Amani Centre where the idea started; colleagues at Tumaini University Makumira, Mbeya Centre where the idea was further developed; Mr. Baraka Nkoko for reading and nourishing the language and concepts of the first draft, and my home mentors for their moral support and encouragement.

I appreciate the concern of non-degree and undergraduate students I taught in the course of my work at the University of Iringa and Tumaini University Makumira Mbeya Centre for their openness to me as they made every effort towards accomplishing their course assignments. I am indebted to the two personal secretaries at Tumaini University Makumira Mbeya Centre: Neema Alex Kapalila and Agnes Syoge Kagelelo, for their tireless work of typing the first draft of the manuscript and its subsequent corrections in the computer for all the drafts that followed. The editors and the typesetters at Wipf and Stock publishers are also worth mentioning for their typesetting and editorial works making this book appear in the form it has now. Their works are excellent! Eventually, I thank and wish God's blessings to all those who provided support in one way or another to fulfill my ambitions for this book.

Chapter 1

INTRODUCTION

Background and Rationale

THE IDEA AND MOTIVATION to write this book is not spontaneous. It originates from my own experience as a university lecturer over the years of my lecturing two courses, "Foundations of Faith and Professional Ethics" and "Introduction to Research Methodology" to non-degree and undergraduate programs. Most students in these programs could hardly understand what entailed academic assignments and write well-organized, well-documented, and well-presented assignments as fulfillments of my semester courses. My experience was supplemented by what other lecturers lamented regarding the ability of such students in writing individual and group assignments for fulfilling the requirements of provided courses. This experience called for the need of a guide book for students in these levels to enable them to have the necessary skills in writing both group and individual assignments.

There are, of course, many good books on research methodology, both electronic and printed. However, most of these books are mainly for advanced students to guide them on how to conduct and document advanced research. They do not lay a foundation for non-degree and undergraduate students to grow within academic writing environments. As a result, when such students reach

Writing Effective Course Assignments

higher levels of studies (postgraduate), where they will be required to write research projects, theses, and dissertations, they feel such tasks to be burdens because of a lack of proper foundation.

As John Biggam writes, "Writing [academic assignments] need not be a guessing-game. Writing [academic assignments] that will achieve pass marks or—even better—excellent marks is as much a technique as it is an art."[1] My experience as I studied undergraduate and postgraduate programs in the past years indicated that the proper foundation for an art of academic writing mostly emanates from class assignments provided by lecturers and students commitment to write them effectively. When students practice writing skills in groups and in individual works assigned seriously, the foundation for becoming excellent writers develops. When students reach the higher levels of their studies, writing becomes something normal; it becomes an art developed in the course of time as such students become involved in writing course assignments. The experience gained from the academic lives of non-degree students and their struggles to survive in their academic writing has been the main inspiration for my initiative to write this book. Therefore, this book is important in various ways: first, it covers the gap left between inexperienced non-degree students in matters of research and effective writing at the bottom, and the flowery research methodology books at the top, with the aim of developing the art of writing to students pursuing non-degree and undergraduate courses.

Second, it exposes and directs students towards constructing credible academic works to be possibly developed further into publishable forms. A well-written course assignment can later be developed into a journal article, a book chapter, or a monograph for publication. There is a need to have course assignments that are later published for wider readership instead of assignments that are just for acquiring semester grades and being shelved at home. This need for developing and publishing academically written course assignments in various academic forms makes this book

---

1 Biggam, *Succeeding with Your Master's Dissertation*, 13.

INTRODUCTION

ultimately important for helping students develop and disseminate knowledge that emanates from class works.

Third, since there is hardly a book available to guide students towards writing effective course assignments for universities and colleges, it is possible that students have been doing their assignments depending on either their own creativity, the directives from their course lecturers, or instructions provided to them by lecturers of the communication skills course. There has been no consistent and comprehensive way or material to guide students to engage in academic writing that leads to publishable course assignments. This book provides a guiding framework to course lecturers towards the better supervision and evaluation of assignments from their students.

Fourth, since writing course assignments involves intensive reading of literatures in a particular issue in the semester course, as will be seen in the chapters inside the book, this book is important because it argues for the necessity of students to find possible areas for future specialization. It also encourages students to think critically and develop their academic and professional, critical, argumentative curiosity. This means that students who will master writing well-argued and well-presented assignments will be successful in most of their course assignments provided by their lecturers and producing various professional writings after graduating. Rise B. Axelrod and Charles R. Cooper rightly put it: "Because writing encourages us to think critically and helps us learn, it also makes a significant contribution to academic and professional success. Students whose writing is logically organized, well-supported, and inventive usually do well in courses throughout the curriculum."[2] Therefore, writing well-thought course assignments following the guides provided in this book will make students skilled writers preparing themselves for writing theses and dissertations in postgraduate studies and various professional papers in their work places.

Fifth, this book provokes lecturers in universities and colleges to explore its deficiencies, as they use it, which will probably lead them towards developing other more effective guides for writing

---

2 Axelrod, and Cooper, *The St.Martin's Guide to Writing*, 3.

course assignments than this one. Since one core function of any college or university is research and dissemination of knowledge, course assignments have to be part of such precious endeavors. The development of manuals and books should aim at enhancing students to write academically credible course assignments not only for acquiring good semester grades, but also for advancing and disseminating academic knowledge.

Intended Audience

As stated in the above paragraph, this book is mainly for students of non-degree and undergraduate programs in universities and colleges to whom assignments are prerequisites for fulfilling the requirements of their semester courses. Non-degree and undergraduate students will find this book useful because it covers most of what they have to know in their level to equip them towards being efficient and effective academic writers. However, other students in higher academic levels may also find this book helpful in reminding them of their responsibility to write well-organized, well-documented, and well-presented academic assignments. For higher level students, the book does not guarantee complete coverage of what they have to accomplish in what is required of them; however, it provides useful introductory skills before they consult other books on research and academic writing to cover their required skills.

Organization and Synopsis

To accomplish its goal, the book is presented in seven chapters. This introduction describes what the book is all about and the rationale for presenting it in this way. Chapter two presents the politics of the process of writing your assignment report. It discusses the various stages you will have to pass through as you move towards a systematically developed assignment; which include: formulating a topic from the assignment question provided by the lecturer, mapping a strategy to investigate the problem within the topic, formulating the research question to investigate the problem in the topic, prior

INTRODUCTION

assembling of relevant materials that will be investigated, constructing a tentative thesis to guide the investigation process, doing the actual investigation using the assembled materials, turning and refining the tentative thesis into an actual thesis statement, and writing the actual first draft of your assignment.

The third chapter deals with issues of documentation. It describes the meaning of the concept of documentation, the reasons for documenting sources you use in your writing, what is done in the documentation process, and some commonly used documenting styles.

Chapter four grapples with the question of "using sources" when writing an assignment. Using sources is different from documenting sources. The chapter defines what entails using sources, discusses integral and non-integral citations of sources, the way reporting verbs are used in citations, the role played by citations in the writing process, and how to show additions and omissions in direct quotations.

Chapter five wrestles with how well you will present your ideas in an assignment. It discusses the way you should formulate the introduction, the body and conclusion parts of your assignment in order for your academic readers to enjoy reading. The chapter illustrates some special sentences used in academic writing for each of the above-listed parts of the assignment. Moreover, issues of unity, coherence, and support are dealt with in this chapter to show their contribution towards a well-presented assignment report.

Chapter six discusses how you should construct an informed argument. It elaborates the meaning of argument and outlines the types of arguments in academic writing. With relevant examples, the chapter discusses the main components of a well-constructed argument, discusses what entails an informed argument, the common fallacies in argumentation committed by most assignment report writers, and how to avoid biases in argumentation.

Chapter seven ends the book with a summary of key issues presented in the entire book. It is my conviction that the book will be of help to the target people to facilitate their understanding and practice of academic writing in their respective fields of study.

Chapter 2

WRITING YOUR ASSIGNMENT

Chapter Learning Objectives

IN THE COURSE OF studying the theme of this chapter, students should be able to:

1. *Define the concepts of writing, research paper, and course assignment.*
2. *Construct an assignment topic (with a problem in it) from the lecturer's assignment question.*
3. *Formulate research questions from the research topics they formulated*
4. *Prepare their own search strategies for materials to use in writing their assignments.*
5. *Assemble relevant materials using the search strategy prepared.*
6. *Construct tentative theses of fact and of action to guide their investigations; and change the tentative theses into thesis statements.*
7. *Use the relevant materials assembled to write the first drafts of their assignments.*

WRITING YOUR ASSIGNMENT

Introduction

The first and most important thing you have to know as a student of College and higher-learning institution is the meanings of concepts: *writing, course assignment,* and *research paper.* Why should you know these three concepts in the course of reading this book? It is because this book is concerned with the way you can write, and write successfully and effectively. In this case, defining these three terms and the way they relate to one another provides a useful background to what will follow in subsequent chapters.

What is writing?

Scholars on writing Mathukutty M. Manippally and Badrinarayan Shankar Pawar clearly indicate the importance of the question of writing. We quote them before providing the meaning of writing: "It is not enough to be smart and knowledgeable; we have to demonstrate our knowledge and insights through writing whether we are students or scholars. Otherwise we would be like wild flowers—perhaps the most beautiful on earth with exquisite scent, but unseen, unsmelt and unsung. That is as bad as being nonexistent."[1] In the above quotation, scholars indicate the importance of nurturing yourself in the scholarly writing environment and growing up as writer. What they say is quite clear: no scholar will claim to be alive without writing! An academic who does not write is as good as a dead scholar despite the number of degrees he or she holds! Therefore, writing is a call to you to demonstrate your existence, beautiful smell, and being seen and heard as an emerging academic in your field.

Now, what is writing? According to Baraka M. Nkoko, "Writing is the act of drawing letters of alphabet of a given language, symbols and markers on a plain surface, especially a piece of paper in order to communicate message."[2] The drawn letters stand as symbols to represent sounds of that language derived

---

1 Monippally & Pawar, *Academic Writing,* xiii.
2 Nkoko, *Practical Communication Skills,* 254.

spontaneously within the culture of people who speak that particular language. The letters, as symbols, are drawn systematically to build up meaningful units (sentences, paragraphs and chapters) for the author to convey the intended message. In this case, writing symbols (letters of alphabet) on a plain surface represents the sounds of those letters which could be spoken with one's mouth.[3]

Writing, in the sense of this book, does not just involve drawing letters on a particular plain surface; rather, it has to do with more than that activity. It is an activity whereby the one drawing the letters—called the writer—uses particular skills and agreed conventions to arrange those letters in a particular meaningful pattern to convey the intended message. Since writing involves a *skill to draw letters using agreed conventions*, it has to be learned and exercised following the conventions of a particular community. You have to learn the conventions guiding your community on what entails meaningful communication of written message. This means that writing is not just a gift bestowed by God upon an individual; rather, it is something you have to learn and practice.[4]

We should emphasize here that writing is not something simple. It is something you have to struggle with it, especially if you are a beginner. Scholars Debbie Epstein, Jane Kenway and Rebeca Boden warn us about writing when they say: "Writing does get easier with practice, but it is always hard work and even the most experienced of writers have bad days in which they write one paragraph.... Anyone who says that they find writing easy may simply be trying to undermine your confidence. Because [strictly speaking] it is hard, don't be ashamed about having to ask for help."[5] Therefore, there is no one who is an expert in writing, who just has to stay sedentarily waiting for things to happen on paper. Writing is like playing a musical instrument or driving a car. You have to practice your musical instrument or driving your car everyday in order to be perfect in those activities. Likewise, to be a good writer,

---

3 Ibid.
4 Ibid.
5 Epstein, Kenway & Boden, *Writing for Publication*, 17.

WRITING YOUR ASSIGNMENT

you have to read extensively from the materials written by other people and practice effectively on your skills for writing your own.

Types of Essays to Write

After defining the concept of *writing* in the above paragraphs, we now turn our attention to what you are supposed to write. As a student of non-degree and undergraduate, you are supposed to write assignments in the form of *essays*. According to Susan Anker, there are various types of essays and each one depends on your purpose for writing it. Some of such essay types are the following:[6] The first is a *narrative essay* which tells a story about a certain event, or your experience about a particular issue in life. The main purpose of narrative essays is to tell your audience what happened (event) or to entertain them. Consider the paragraph below:

> But I did not want to shoot the elephant. I watched him beating his bunch of grass against his kneels, with that preoccupied grandmotherly air that elephants have. It seemed to me that it would be murder to shoot him. At that age I was not squeamish about killing animals, but I had never shot an elephant and never wanted to. (Somehow it always seems worse to kill a *large* animal.) Besides, there was the beast's owner to be considered. Alive, the elephant was worth at least a hundred pounds; dead, he would only be worth the value of his tusks, five pounds, possibly. But I had got to act quickly. I turned to some experienced—looking Burmans who had been there when we arrived, and asked them how the elephant had been behaving. They all said the same thing: he took no notice no notice of you if you left him alone, but he might charge if you went too close to him.[7]

The second is *illustration essays* which provide examples in order to show, explain, or prove about the point you are trying to make.

---

6 Anker, *Real Essays with Readings*, 147–315, cf. Tibbet & Tibbetts, *Strategies of Rhetoric*, 38–88.

7 Paragraph is taken from Sonia Brownell Orwell as quoted in Baker, *The Practical Stylist*, 30–31.

Always in this type of essays the main point you make is backed up by as many examples as possible. Consider the following example:

> Teaching a new language to grown up people is more difficult than teaching it to children. This point can be illustrated by examples from two classes. The first class comprised of adults whose language of instruction was Kiswahili, the lingua franca of Tanzania. When English was introduced in this class as a subject, teachers complained that students found it difficult studying the language. The second class comprised of kindergarten pupils whose language of instruction was also Kiswahili. English was also introduced in this class as a subject. Teachers enjoyed teaching this class because pupils became conversant with the language as the teaching went on. The two classes indicate that the age of learners is an important factor to consider when teaching a foreign language.

The third is *Description essays* which translate your experience into words. The experience translated may not be of human beings; it may be of places, or of things. The clear impression about your experience, which you put into words, creates a description. Consider the following example:

> Three young women, and one of mature years, left their homes of wealth, and comfort ... and their beautiful native State of Washington, for dark S. China. Two of these three young women died there soon after from tropical diseases—and this was the tragic fate of many of these unprepared missionaries, who refused to take medicines, not wanting to show lack of faith in divine healing.[8]

This paragraph is a description because it tries to recount the experiences of Pentecostal missionaries as they moved from the United States of America to missionary areas and were unwilling to take hospital medicines, but depended only on prayers for healing.

The fourth is *Process analysis essays* which explain the way things happen. This means that they explain how you can do things in the way that your readers can also do for themselves; or

---

8 Akoko, "Ask and You will be Given," 51.

WRITING YOUR ASSIGNMENT

how things work in order for your readers to understand or do them for themselves. Consider the following example:

> The Chub, though he eat well thus dressed, yet as he is usually dressed he does not: he is objected against, not only for being full of small forked bones, dispersed through all his body, but that he eats waterfish, and that the flesh of him is not firm, but short and tasteless. The French esteem him so mean as to call him *un Vilain;* nevertheless he may be so dressed as to make him very good meat: as namely, if he be a large Chub, then dress him thus: First scale him, and then wash him clean, and then take out his guts; and to that end make the hole as little and near to his gills as you may conveniently, and especially make clean his throat from the grass and weeds that are usually in it, for if that not be clean, it will make him to taste very sour. Having so done, put some sweet herbs into his belly; and then tie it with two or three splinters to a spit, and roast him, with good store of salt mixed with it. Being thus dressed, you will find him a much better dish of meat than you or most folk, even than Anglers themselves, do imagine; for this dries up the fluid watery humor with which all Chubs do abound.[9]

The fifth is *classification essays which* categorize things into groups. The categorization is mainly based on similar characteristics. It can be types of behaviors, types of movies, or classes of animals, birds, etc. Consider one of the classification paragraphs below:

> Women [in the nineteenth century] were not accorded what the twentieth century considers basic human rights. Politically women were virtual nonentities. Their contributions were confined largely to the domestic realm. They could not secure employment in the occupation of their choice, and higher education was practically closed to them. In addition, they were not only denied the right to vote; they were, socially and individually, perceived under the jurisdiction of men. Once married, a woman lost all claim to any property she had previously owned; it was

---

9 These paragraphs are taken from Sonia Brownell Orwell as quoted in Baker, *The Practical Stylist*, 33.

transferred to her husband. She had legal claims neither to her own body nor to her children in the event of divorce.[10]

The sixth is *definition essays* which tell what a term, concept or issue means in a particular context. It should be in mind that various fields of study and life contexts have various terms and concepts used by people who belong to those contexts or fields. Definition essays are extended explanations that aim at making clear about a term or concept to an audience which do not belong to the particular context or field. It can also be a further elaboration of the concept to those who belong to the context for them to know more about it. Consider one of the definition paragraphs below:

> The term *leitourgia* in classical Greek described the performance of a special honorific service for the state, such as, for instance, outfitting a worship, or providing a choir for a theatrical performance at a major ceremony. The honor dimension was important to the term. By the second century B.C. the word was used in popular language for priestly service in the worship of the gods. In the Septuagint it was used for the Hebrew *sharath* to designate participation in the divine worship, either as an officiant or as a worshiper. While in the New Testament the more common term for serving is *diaconia*, by Hippolytus' time *leitourgia* and *munus* were the accepted terms for the performance of Christian worship, especially the Eucharist. These words conveyed the idea of the prestige of the one who could officiate in the church service.[11]

The seventh is *comparison and contrast essays* which focus on showing the similarities and differences among objects, people, ideas, etc. Your main aim in this type of essays is to show the way things are alike or different. You can write an essay to compare things, to show their differences, or show both similarities and differences.

> In the evangelical Christian community, the issue of headship/submission/equality lies in the heart of the

---

10 Worley Quoted in Vyhmeister, *Quality Research Papers*, 118.
11 Augusburger Quoted in Vyhmeister, *Quality Research Papers*, 116—117.

WRITING YOUR ASSIGNMENT

> fundamental differences between the two major proactive groups in the ordination debate. The Council on Biblical Manhood and Womanhood, representing those who oppose women's ordination, ultimately bases its biblical argument on the premise that the divine plan in creation affirmed the equality of the sexes in spiritual status but included role distinctions involving the headship of man over woman..... Those holding this position have been referred to as "patriarchalists," "hierchalists" or (their preferred self- designation) "complementarians." The second group, Christians for Biblical Equality, representing evangelicals who support women's ordination, argue that the divine plan at Creation affirmed full equality of the sexes without any male headship or female submission.... Those holding this view have been referred to as "Christian feminists" or (their preferred self-designation) "egaritarians."[12]

The eighth is *cause and effect essays which* state the reasons for what has resulted, or state the effect for a particular cause. Here your aim will be to show the relationship between the causer and the result. You can decide to write about what causes, on what is the result, or on both of them in one essay.

> Even in the religious arena, [nineteenth-century] women were limited. Most churches did not ordain women and either prohibited or frowned upon women speaking in public. Because a large sector of society perceived the church as responsible for the denigration of women, many elements in the women's movement became hostile to it. For example, powerful crusader Elizabeth Gage called the church the bulwark of women's slavery. For her, no entity was more offensive than organized religion. For this reason, freedom from religious orthodoxy became crucial to feminist leadership.[13]

The ninth is *argument essays which* take a position about an issue, provides reasons for taking that position, and backing them

---

12 Davison Quoted in Vyhmeister, *Quality Research Papers*, 117.
13. Worley Quoted in Vyhmeister, *Quality Research Papers*, 117–118.

up with appropriate evidence. The main purpose of this type of essays can be to convince or persuade readers. Here, all types of papers: research papers, journal articles, book chapters, theses, dissertations, and course assignments belong to this group of essays because they require you to take a position and defend that position with reasons and evidence. Consider the following example:

> For a developing country like Tanzania, where there are only few individuals who own computers and have access to internet connectivity, mobile phone can be a vital ICT tool for both teaching and learning (Traxler and Kukulska-Hulme 2005). This is due to the fact that, mobile phones have nearly similar utilities as those of a computer, iPad, TV, camera and other ICT tools. Through the use of mobile phones, both teachers and students can manage to record and listen to audio or video files, send SMS, access internet, chat (both synchronous and asynchronous), watch movies/video, carry out a teleconferencing and access any other synchronous and asynchronous communications (Kasumuni 2011; Traxler and Kukulska-Hulme 2005). As long as the mobile phones are simple, easy and handy; they offer a vital opportunity for both teaching and learning flexibility (Collis and Moonen 2001). Using a mobile phone, students can easily learn from any place whenever convenient and suitable to them; like in buses, at home, in gardens and parks, even at market places. Such an impressive flexibility can neither be offered by a computer (laptop), iPod, digital camera, TV, Radio, nor any other ICT tool known in educational learning processes. Mobile phones are normally carried in pockets and handbags. Thus, we do have them wherever we are and we can use them whenever we want. In this study mobile phones are considered as vital tools for both teaching and learning processes that can best serve as alternative device for overcoming the shortage of technological tools in schools in Tanzania and enhance students' learning from anywhere and at anytime.[14]

---

14 Paragraph is from Kafyulilo, "Access, Use and Perceptions."

WRITING YOUR ASSIGNMENT

The above paragraph is an example of argumentative essay because it tries to convince the readers about the use of mobile phones as tools for teaching.

Course Assignments and Research Papers

Having stated what you are supposed to write in the above paragraphs, we now turn to course assignments and research papers as argument essays mostly written for academic purposes. As a non-degree and undergraduate student, you are expected to write *argument essays*. In academic writing, argument essays for non-degree and undergraduate students are of two types: *research papers* and *course assignments*. What are research papers and course assignments? In his book called *Writing academic Papers*, Elia Shabani Mligo categorizes both research papers and course assignments as *academic papers*. He defines an academic paper as a "written document resulting from systematic or scientific investigation of a particular phenomenon."[15] What is important in Mligo's definition is that both research papers and course assignments are "assignments." In other words, both are "academic paper assignments."[16] However, in this book, a research paper will refer to a long academic paper assignment to fulfill the requirements for undergraduate studies, or their equivalent, submitted at the end of the program duration; and a course assignment will refer to a term paper of a particular course or any other paper assigned to a student as part of the requirement of that course in a particular semester submitted within the respective semester.

Following Mligo's definitions above, we may understand that both course assignments and research papers have an element of "*research.*" It means that you cannot write a convincing course assignment or research paper without conducting research. What, then, is research? The term "*research*" has acquired various definitions, complex and simple ones, satisfactory to one reader

---

15 Mligo, *Writing Academic Papers*, 14.
16 Ibid., 15.

Writing Effective Course Assignments

and unsatisfactory to another. For our purpose, in this book, it is satisfactory to define research as a systematic investigation of a particular topic (theme or idea) which is not known by yourself, and you do not have an experience about it, in order to know it.[17]

When we say that "research is systematic" we mean that writing a term paper, research paper, or any other academic assignment does not only require you to read other people's works and summarize what they say; rather, it also requires you to "evaluate and interpret the ideas explored in your sources and to formulate your own ideas."[18] This is what is called *critical thinking and argumentation*. You have to think about ideas you read from your sources, evaluate them, and argue your own case following the knowledge you have gained from these ideas.

Laurie G. Kirszner and Stephen R. Mandell analyze the following issues you have to take into account when you undergo research for your course assignment and research paper:

- Moving from assignment question to researchable topic,
- Mapping a strategy you will use to investigate the problem in your topic,
- Formulating a research question to address the problem in the topic,
- Assembling materials (bibliography) related to the problem you want to address,
- Developing a tentative thesis to guide your investigation
- Conducting the actual research to collect information in order to answer the question stated
- Constructing an outline to help write the assignment, and writing the first draft of your assignment using the collected information.[19]

---

17 Cf. Kirszner & Mandell, *The Concise Wadsworth handbook*, 334.
18 Ibid.
19 Kirszner & Manddell, *The Concise Wadsworth Handbook*.

WRITING YOUR ASSIGNMENT

These are the issues which we will discuss in this chapter; and therefore, we will begin with the way you have to move from the assignment question to a topic for investigation.

Moving from Assignment Question to Topic for Research

Normally, the lecturer provides a question to work on it as an assignment. He or she may provide a theme or idea for you to work on within a specific time. This is called *assignment question, theme or idea*. Alternatively, the lecturer may require you to formulate the question, theme, or idea for your assignment under his or her instruction. In whatever case, the lecturer will require from you a sensitively and diligently articulated work from the question, idea or theme you have.

You require moving from the question, idea, or theme provided by your lecturer or formulated by yourself to a formal researchable topic. To move from assignment question, idea, or theme to a formal researchable topic, first you will have to understand the nature of the assignment and what it entails: has your lecturer provided you a question, an idea, or a theme to work on it? Has the lecturer required that you formulate your own question, theme or idea? What is the purpose of the assignment question, idea or theme provided or formulated by you? Who is the audience for your final assignment report, your fellow students, the lecturer, or both of them? What assumption do you have about the knowledge of your audience in regard to the question, theme or idea you intend to work on it? What support do you anticipate to have from your lecturer or your fellow students to accomplish your assignment task? These questions are important to consider when you attempt to formulate a topic for the assignment question, theme, or idea.

Richard Bullock and Francine Weinberg provide a good piece of advice, "If your topic [or theme] is assigned, read the assignment carefully to make sure you understand what it asks you to do. If the assignment offers only broad guidelines, identify the requirements

17

Writing Effective Course Assignments

and range of possibilities, and define your topic within those constraints."[20] This statement means that understanding what the assignment requires you to do is an important step towards dealing with it in order to have an adequate assignment topic.

Similarly, Ronald Lundford and Bill Bridges advise that once your lecturer provides you an assignment question to work on it, your first step is to identify the primary purpose of your lecturer. What does your lecturer want you to do? In other words, what is the task that your lecturer requires you to accomplish in that question, theme, or idea? According to Lundford and Bridges, one way to understand the task which is directed by your lecturer in the assignment question is to identify the main terms used in the question. The key terms used will show the task you are supposed to accomplish in that assignment question, theme, or idea. Therefore, in the words of Lundford and Bridges, "For all assigned topics, identify the key terms of the assignment [question, theme, or idea] and use those key terms as an initial guide in completing the assignment."[21] Consider the following assignment provided by the lecturer:

> Write a 10 to 12 pages paper to evaluate on the use of internet. This paper will be presented in class and marked separately after reworking on the comments from your fellow students.

The thing you have to do when moving from assignment to topic is formulating a *focused topic* with a *research problem* in it. In the above assignment, the lecturer provided a broad idea—"the use of internet"—to work on; and the key verb in the question statement is "evaluate." Here, the lecturer wants you to evaluate the use of internet. This is his or her purpose. You have to formulate a "focused research topic" that identifies the problem or issue you want to deal with among the many possible issues contained in that idea. The focus of the topic you formulate should be evaluation, which is in line with the purpose of your lecturer. Consider

---

20 Bullock, Richard & Wenberg, *The Little Seagull Handbook*, 68–69.
21 Lundford and Bridges, *The Longwood Guide to Writing*, 10.

WRITING YOUR ASSIGNMENT

the following example of a more focused topic from the above general idea provided by the lecturer in the above assignment:

> An Evaluation of the use of Internet among Primary School Children in Tanzania

In the above-formulated topic, you have focused your general idea by narrowing it down. Instead of dealing with the whole *animal*, you now deal with an organ within the big *animal*. Here you are no longer working with the whole general idea of "the use of internet," which you can hardly manage. You are now working with internet use among primary school children in Tanzania. In focusing your topic, you have provided a specific group (primary school children) and a context (Tanzania) to your provided general idea. You can also focus further to deal with a very small part of an organ of the *animal*. Consider the following more focused topic:

> The use of Internet Services among Primary School Children in Mbeya City, Tanzania

Here you are no longer working with all primary schools in Tanzania to evaluate on their use of internet, but only primary schools in which are in Mbeya City in Tanzania as a representative sample. You can still focus further than that depending on what you will find easier for you to work on. You have to bear in mind that the more you narrow your topic and focus on a small issue in an animal, the more credible and detail will be your work; and the more unfocused is your topic, the more superficial you will be, and the less credible your work will be. Therefore, narrowing your topic and focusing on a small issue is important in order to write a detailed and well-researched assignment.

According to Carol Collier Kuhlthau, the topic you formulate for a course assignment from the assignment question, theme or idea should at least meet the following four criteria:

- See whether the topic draws your interest to research on it
- See whether the topic satisfies the needs of or requirements which your instructor would like you to fulfill as per the assignment question, theme, or idea.

- See whether it will be possible for you to collect and put together the collected information within the given time of the assignment.

- See whether you can collect enough information to enable you answer your question in the topic you formulated.[22]

The above-listed criteria are important because the formulated research topic fulfils important tasks: telling your readers what they are going to see in your assignment, enticing your readers and building in them an urge to read it, and helping you in your search for literature in both the library and internet.

Mapping a Search Strategy to use in Investigating the Problem

You have moved from the general idea of the assignment question, ideas, or theme (the whole animal), i.e., you have understood your assignment and formulated a focused research topic that meets Kuhlthau's four criteria listed above. Now, you have to plan for the search strategy to deal with the problem within your topic. Here you state how you will work with your assignment, or how you will gather information regarding the assignment you have. What you mainly do in this part is to state the way you will review other people's studies/works and gather information for your assignment. This is what is called *Literature Search*.[23] Biggan, quoting Gash, defines literature search as "a systematic and thorough search of all

---

22. Kuhlthau, *Teaching the Library Research Process*, 34–37.

23 The word "literature" comes from the Latin word "*litteratus*" (plural: *literati*) which means "letter." As the days went on, the word was used to refer to "a man of letters," a man educated with a restricted educational opportunity, being well acquainted with books. Afterwards, the word was used to refer to a learned person, a person who can read and write. A literate person is the one who knows how to read and write and the illiterate person is the one who does not know how to read and write. Currently, the word is also used to refer to any published or unpublished piece of writing which the researcher consults as the bases for his or her research (See Biggam, *Succeeding with Your Master's Dissertation*, 41). This last meaning is what the word "literatures" refers to in this book.

types of published literature in order to identify as many items as possible that are relevant to a particular topic.

An effective search of literature in whatever form—books, journal articles, reports, official publications, conference papers, theses, etc.—requires a structured approach."[24] To make the search for literatures systematic, we usually select an appropriate topic, define the main terms or concepts within the selected topic, set the parameters or boundaries in which the search will fall, select the sources of information and analyze them to obtain information required. In doing that systematic search, we normally start searching for the more general literatures and end up searching for the more specific ones. The more general literatures provide an overview of the topic and the more specific ones focus on the problem you want to deal with.

We should emphasize here that you do not gather any information at this stage of mapping a search strategy; you just outline the search strategy to deal with your problem in the narrowed topic. The search strategy will depend on the nature of the assignment. It deals with the how of your assignment. How will you go about accomplishing your assignment? It means that some assignments may need library materials (books, journal articles, and so on) while others may require you to conduct fieldwork. In whatever the case, you have to outline *how* you will work on the topic.

Formulating a Research Question to address the Problem

You have now explored the topic through the various literatures—the more general and the more focused ones, and have set out the search strategy for literatures in order to deal with the topic. You have to formulate the question that you will be answering in your assignment. The question you formulate will focus on the problem in your topic, and will determine the type of literatures to use in

---

24 Biggam, *Succeeding with Your Mster's Dissertation*, 41.

your collection of materials. Consider the following research question from the previously formulated research topic:

- Topic: *The use of Internet among Primary School Children at Mbeya City in Tanzania.*
- Research Question: *Why should Primary School Children in Mbeya City use Internet Services at this Era?*

The above question leads you towards searching for *reasons* on the importance of using internet to children in primary schools in Mbeya city. Hence, the research question you have formulated will be the starting point for your research proper.

Assembling Relevant Materials

After you have set out the search strategy for assembling materials and formulated your research question, you should now assemble the materials you have to read in detail to search for answers for the question. Moreover, you may have to go to the field to search for answers from the real situation. Therefore, assembling valuable and more insightful materials to read, or doing a thorough survey in the field will easy the gathering of information and writing the assignment report.

In assembling materials for your assignment, the following information must be included for each document to assemble in order for you to remember properly when compiling the final bibliography:

For Books: Full names of the author (s), Title of the book (in italics), City where it was published, publisher, date of publication, call number in that particular library, possible pages to read in detail, and your evaluation of the information for you to remember when you read it in detail to collect information. However, it should be noted that the procedure will depend on the citation style you have decided to select: whether APA, Chicago, MLA, and so on. Moreover, it should be noted that some books are written by several authors and others are edited. When collecting materials, the above aspects have to be considered. Consider the following book by a single author:

> Elia Shabani Mligo, *Elements of African Traditional Religion: A Textbook for Students of Comparative Religion*, Eugene OR.: Wipf and stock/Resource, 2013.

Evaluation

> This book deals with key elements of the African Traditional Religion (ATR). Attention will be paid to pages 69–90. These pages evaluate the practice of ATR among the Bena tribe of Njombe.

For Journal Articles: Full names of the author (s), Title of the Article (with or without quotation marks depending on style), Title of the Journal (in italics), volume, Number, date of publication of the journal, and the pages which the article covers within the journal. Consider the following example:

> Elia Shabani Mligo, "Jesus Christ, a Compassionate Companion: Christological Reflection in the Time of HIV/AIDS." *Acta Theologica*, Volume 34, Number 2 (2014), pp. 60—76.

Evaluation

> This article is about the views of people living with HIV/AIDS on the theme of stigma. I will read the whole article to explore their views and incorporate the views in my assignment.

If the journal article is downloaded from the internet, you have to provide the Uniform Resource Locator (URL) and the date you downloaded it. You do the same listing for any material you think to be important for your assignment.

The question is: How can you know that a particular book or journal article is important in your assignment? It is tempting to collect or list materials that will prove to be useless in your future work. To avoid this temptation, it is advised that you read thoroughly the book chapters, journal articles, or sections relevant to your assignments and collect relevant information in the form of paraphrases, summaries or direct quotations as you read. After that you should include the book or journal article in the list for future references. By so doing, you save time by doing two things, i.e., *reading* and *listing* the materials in the bibliography instead of listing first and then reading them later. My experience shows that most students who do not consider the two things simultaneously have cited their sources in the main bodies of their assignments without including them in the list of references or bibliography at the end. This is one of the academic grave mistakes because it evokes suspicion to the reader of your assignment regarding its credibility.

Generally, the book or material you collect for your assignment will be important and useful if:

1. *It treats your topic in a considerable detail.* If the book devotes a chapter or several sections discussing issues related to your topic, it is considered useful. It will be not useful enough if it just has a footnote or a small section about your assignment topic.

2. *It is recent.* If the source is recently published, it is more likely that it has recent information about the problem you deal with in your assignment. Using more recent sources will help you avoid duplicating what other people have just done. It will help you contribute new inputs in dealing with the problem in your topic. In this case, it will make your readers acquire new knowledge and evaluate their old ideas about the problem you have investigated.

3. *It is reliable.* If the source is published, and for an expert audience, is most reliable. Scholarly publications such as books and journal articles are more reliable than popular publications focusing on general readers such as general books, newspapers, and most Internet sources. Therefore, using reliable sources strengthens your argument and its reliability.

The reliability of the source you collect will greatly determine the reliability of your argument. According to Ann Raimes, *scholarly* materials are in most cases reliable for using in academic writing. The source you consult will be academically reliable if it has most of the following academic criteria:

1. It is written using a formal academic language and uses a formal way of presenting its ideas recognized in your discipline.
2. It is written by academic authors, not by journalists writing in popular newspapers, while referring to the works of other scholars to substantiate their claims. Their references are clearly noted in in-text citations, footnotes, or endnotes.
3. It has references, works cited, or bibliography at the end of the work to demonstrate the author's use of other people's works to generate knowledge.
4. It presents original research and interpretation of research findings, and not merely a summary of other people's works. The original research is published in academic books or specialized journals.
5. It describes the scientific method used for research to produce it, or the review of related literatures as a base for producing it.[25]

All of the above stated criteria will help you to distinguish between what is scholarly and what is not scholarly source among the many documents you will consult for your assignment. Again, you have to consult reliable sources to draw your evidence to make your argument strong, reliable, and convincing.

The evidence you use in writing your assignment is not for mere filling in the space of your assignment. According to Diana Hacker and Nancy Sommer it has the following functions:[26]

- It establishes the rationale for your argument. You can cite sources as evidence to show why your assignment topic is worth dealing with. In this case, the evidence you cite will provide the compelling background and context for the problem you want to study.

25 Raimes, *Pocket Keys for Writers*, 41–42.
26 Hacker & Sommer, *The Bedford Handbook*, 687–688.

Writing Effective Course Assignments

- It helps you define the terms and concepts you use in your assignment. The readers of your assignment will better understand the meaning of a concept or term if you back up your definition with an authority (evidence). You can quote the source directly, paraphrase or summarize it.
- It strengthens the claims you make. Any claim you make in each paragraph should be accompanied by reasons and evidence. The more reliable and appropriate evidence you use to support your claim (thesis) the stronger your argument becomes, and vice versa. This means that evidence will support your position on an issue you argue for.
- It provides the voice of other opposing perspectives in your assignment. It shows that there are other views which are against your own point of view. Giving the opposing evidence a voice in your assignment will enable you to either accept or refute it with stronger evidence.

Biggam asserts that most students face problems in the writing process. Such problems include: where to get the appropriate literatures as sources of information for their documentations, how to provide a correct reference of a particular source in their works, how to conduct an appropriate review of the literature searched, and how to organize the literature review into an adequate and convincing manner.[27]

The sources for your assignment should be searched for; they will not just come to you by chance. As Biggam clearly notes:

> By all means type keywords into your Internet browser (use Google Scholar) but also visit the university library, look at past dissertations, read relevant journals, get hold of recently published conference proceedings related to your topic, and follow up the references supplied in your lecture and seminar hand-outs. The material you need do not appear all at once; rather, you will discover that one source will lead to another, one author directing you to another, one article referring to another article that

27 Biggam, *Succeeding with Your Master's Dissertation*, 74.

may be of use to you, and so on. Collecting literature sources is an accumulative process that requires patience and perseverance in equal measure.[28]

Generally, there is no simple means to get materials for review; you have to unearth them where they are. There is no simple means to review the literature without using your energy and brain to read through the selected literatures analytically and critically while thinking on the most convenient logic to present your review for readers to understand what you focus on (the main objectives of your assignment).

Always remember that the way you review the literatures enables your readers to test you whether you have read extensively about your selected topic, whether you are capable of evaluating the sources you consult, and whether you are capable of referencing accurately the sources you consult following the agreed referencing styles.

Constructing a Tentative Thesis Statement to guide your Investigation

After assembling materials relevant to your constructed topic and research question, you cannot start collecting information for your assignment by just using the broad formulated topic. You have to formulate a *thesis* to guide your study of literatures. A thesis is the main idea which your assignment endeavors to support as you continue with research. It represents your position (conviction or opinion) about an issue clearly and directly before doing research. It is a tentative answer to the research question you formulated previously. The main function of the thesis is to guide you in your search for answers to the question from the literatures you collected and the writing of your assignment report. This means that the thesis is the main idea which holds you moving, and is the one you believe as being true. In defending this thesis, you answer the research question.

28 Ibid.

When you have the thesis in your mind, you have to put that thesis into a well-understood sentence. Doing that, you construct a statement for your thesis. A thesis statement is a one-sentence description of your idea or position about an arguable issue.[29] After putting it into a sentence it becomes a *tentative thesis statement*. It is called tentative thesis statement because it will possibly be modified in the course of your reading of literatures and the development of ideas in your mind regarding your research problem, the reasons that will be provided, and the biases, prejudices, interests, prior knowledge, and preconceptions of your readers (audience).[30] The tentative thesis is developed from the position, stance, conviction, or opinion you hold about an issue.[31]

There are two types of thesis statements of which you can formulate: the *tentative thesis statement of fact* and the *tentative thesis statement of action*. On the one hand, the tentative thesis statement of fact is a statement that states an existing fact about a phenomenon you intend to study. Consider the following example of tentative thesis statement of fact:

- Topic: *The Use of Internet among Primary School Children in Mbeya City in Tanzania*
- Research Question: *Why should Primary School Children in Mbeya city use internet services at this era?*
- Tentative Thesis Statement of fact: *The use of Internet enables primary school children to cope with the current developments in technology as they grow up.*

---

29 Skwire & Skwire, *Writing with a Thesis*, 3.
30 Kirszner & Mandell, *The Concise Wadsworth Handbook*, 340–341.
31 There is a difference between a *"Thesis"* and a *"Position."* A position is a general or an overall judgment, stance or opinion you have about an issue (e.g., low income generating people face unfair treatments) while a Thesis is specific, strategic, and appeals to readers experience, interests and biases in order to convince them through reasons and evidence (e.g., low income generating people are treated unfairly when buying goods in wholesale shops in Tanzania [thesis of fact], or [low income generating people should be treated fairly when buying goods from wholesale shops in Tanzania [thesis of action]) (cf. Crusius &Channell, *The Aims of Argument* (2010), 223—224).

WRITING YOUR ASSIGNMENT

On the other hand, a thesis statement of action is a statement that directs readers towards an action; it directs them towards effecting a particular change of an existing situation. Therefore, the thesis of action points to the future of a situation. However, it is based on the thesis statement of fact. Consider the following example of tentative thesis statement on the previous research topic and research question:

- Topic: *An Evaluation of the Use of Internet among Primary School Children in Mbeya City in Tanzania*
- Research Question: *What should be done to make Primary School Children in Mbeya city use internet services for them to cope with current developments of this era?*
- Tentative Thesis of Action: *There is a need to provide positive motivation to primary school children in Mbeya City to make them use Internet in order to cope with the current developments in technology as they grow up in this era.*

Therefore, the above stated thesis statements (whether of fact or of action) are the one you will endeavor to defend as being the strongest points for primary school children to use internet services despite the disadvantages that can emerge as a result of their use. Your actual investigation of the collected literatures will be focused on answering the research question, which eventually makes you defend the thesis statement.

Conducting the Actual Investigation

After you have formulated your tentative main point for your assignment topic (thesis), you now have to move towards conducting the actual investigation. Strictly speaking, conducting the actual research is just a continuation of the research process. When talking of "actual research process," we refer to the process whereby you now start collecting information from your assembled materials through note-taking. Note-taking is using your notebook to record the information you get from the intensive literature search to answer your research question. This means that you have to search for the evidence that supports your thesis. The evidence here may be facts from your readings, fieldwork, statistics, definitions, quotations, summaries from your readings, paraphrases, and so on. You have to consult various sources to get the required information to support your thesis. Kirszner and Mandell call this process "doing focused research."[32] In this process, you have to *read* books, journal articles, magazines, newspapers, or conduct fieldwork in the form of interviews, questionnaires, surveys, and so on, to get information for your assignment.

The Process of Reading

What is reading? This question requires an answer before we proceed to the process of reading itself. Reading is an interaction between you and a particular text. Here, a text may be a book, a journal article, a dictionary, a map, a photograph, a situation, a government report, an advertisement, and so on. It is passing your eyes through such scenarios to understand them. These scenarios are not empty scenarios, they contain meaning in them. To try to understand them is to try to unpack the meaning they have as your eyes pass through them.[33] Therefore, reading and understanding should go together. This means that reading, in its real sense, involves understanding as its key point; and reading is different from reciting where understanding is not the main required issue.

In the reading process there is an interaction between you and the text. The text has information and you as reader have a particular knowledge—you are not a *tabula rasa* (an empty headed person) when you approach a text to read. What happens in the process is that the information provided in the text and your knowledge about the information provided come together to produce meaning. Hence, the meaning constructed from one text varies from one person to another because such people, though

---

[32] Kirszner & Mandell, *The Concise Wadsworth Handbook*, 341–346.
[33] Nkoko, *Practical Communication Skills*, 235–237.

WRITING YOUR ASSIGNMENT

reading the same text, differ in their knowledge possession about the information held in the text.[34]

Reading Sources Academically

Reading literary library academic materials (texts) requires you to *read academically*. You cannot manage to read all academic materials you get in whole. Reading academic materials academically is reading with a purpose where you scan what you want to know to fulfill a particular planned academic requirement. For books, you skim and scan the table of contents, the index, the headings and subheadings and carefully discern what is important for your assignment to read in a more detail.[35] For the article, you read the abstract, the headings and subheadings, and carefully discern what is important for your assignment to read in a more detailed manner. For magazines and newspapers, you skim the headlines to discern what article is important for your assignment that you have to read in detail. This way of reading, where you skim and scan specific areas to get the general idea for a particular predetermined purpose is called *Previewing*.

You may photocopy part of the book, article, magazine or newspaper that you find helpful in developing the argument of your assignment. You may also print, save into a file, attach the file and send it to your e-mail address some online materials you find important for your assignment. In whatever the case, remember to add in the list of materials you assembled previously (bibliography) and new materials you did not list before to avoid ommiting from your bibliography the materials you have used inside the report.

---

34 Seyler, *Read, Reason, Write*, 7–9.

35 There is a difference between *skimming* and *scanning* a particular text though both involve not reading the text in whole. You skim the text when you pass through it without having something specific to search for. You scan the text when you have something you need to find in that text.

Types of Sources to Read

Sources of information for your assignment will in most cases depend on the type of assignment provided by your lecturers and the research question you formulate to answer. You have to cite credible sources that make it strong and reliable. Some assignments require you to conduct only library researches while others fieldworks. In whatever the case, sources of information may be *primary* or *secondary* sources. However, for writing a credible and reliable assignment report, you have to stick more to primary sources rather than secondary sources.

On the one hand, *primary sources* include original documents like historical sources (e.g., speeches, meeting minutes, letters, personal biographies, reports from your own eyewitness (observations), reports from interviewees and questionnaires, reports from telephone communications you make with your informants and works of literature. These are called primary sources because they provide you with firsthand information.

On the other hand, *secondary sources* include the interpretations of original documents, interviews, observational notes or questionnaire responses. They are secondary sources because they provide secondhand information. They are sources that depend on other sources, mostly primary sources. Most research reports are secondary sources because they mostly use primary sources as their source of information. When you use such reports for your own report, they become secondary (or tertiary) sources to you. In this case, you can imagine how the information about an issue can be distorted as it passes from one reporter to another. This is one reason why we emphasize your report should mostly depend on primary sources.

Read Sources and Collect Notes Carefully

During actual research, you have to read *carefully* the materials you collected, highlighting the important points by underlining or using a colored pen. You also have to annotate the important points, i.e., writing your responses to what you read in the margins or between the lines of the source, and take notes or record the information in a separate sheet for your assignment. Remember that this is a research stage; it is not a writing stage yet. The notes you take should be as comprehensive as possible for you to use them in the future stages of your assignment. Since you have a clear idea of your topic, question and thesis, you have to collect information that will help you respond to those issues. The notes you take should be placed under particular headings which you imagine will appear in one of the sections for your assignment report. Remember to document the corresponding source of the notes accurately for future use.

Notes for your assignment can be collected in various forms: as direct quotations, as a summary, the whole or part of the source, or as a paraphrase of part or of the whole source. We will discuss the aspects of direct quotation, summary and paraphrase in the next chapter. However, remember to comment on the notes you have taken in your own words before you forget the main idea of what you have read. Consider the following examples of notes and their comments:

1. Direct Quotation
    Initiation Ceremony in Africa

    "The Christology of Jesus as an African master of initiation is located within the cultural realm of African people. Initiations are ritual practices with a meaning within the community which practices them." (Mligo, 2011: 165) Shelf Call No. 232.33

    Comment

    In the above quotation, Mligo expresses the location of initiation rituals in the African context. He mentions circumcision as one example of initiation to emphasize his point. Mligo's location of initiation rituals in Africa is important towards our understanding of ritual practices among human beings of a particular context.

2. Summary Note
The Christology of Jesus Christ as Compassionate Companion

> In chapter seven of his book *"Jesus and the Stigmatized"* Mligo has developed a Christology of Jesus as Compassionate Companion. In doing that, he has compared the Christology with the other existing Christologies in Africa such as: *Jesus as African chief, African ancestor, elder brother, master of initiation, and African healer*. He defines the concept of "compassion" and discusses the way people living with HIV/AIDS portray the image of Jesus as compassionate companion in their reading of texts from the Gospel according to John. He also compares their images with the way Jesus handled the stigmatization of other people and his own stigmatization in the gospel (Mligo, 2011:360-389).

Comment

> Mligo leads us towards a new understanding of the role of Jesus Chris in the Gospel according to John. The important insight in Mligo's chapter is his development of Christology of Jesus as compassionate companion in comparison with the insights of traditional African Christologies.

In the above examples, the three important aspects of a note can be seen: the note itself (whether direct, summary or paraphrase), the documentation, and the comment to show the usefulness of the note in regard to your assignment. The comment clarifies the reasons for recording the information in that note.

Turning the Tentative Thesis Statement into the Final Thesis Statement

Timothy W. Crusius and Carolyn E. Channell state that "A good thesis [statement] grows out of a combination of things: your position, your research, your exploration of reasons to support your position, and your understanding of the audience."[36] After

---

36 Crusius & Channell, *The Aims of Argument*, 225.

WRITING YOUR ASSIGNMENT

you have collected a vast amount of information to support your tentative thesis, have scrutinized the interests, prior knowledge, preconceptions, and biases of your audience, you have to use this information to re-formulate your tentative thesis statement into a final thesis statement. *A final thesis statement for your assignment is a single sentence that states an overall conclusion of the notes you have been collecting from literatures, the position you had when collecting the notes, and the view you have about your audience.* It is the sentence that indicates the direction and scope of the whole assignment. This means that you will have to read the collected notes carefully, review your position, and ascertain the interests and biases of your audience, and re-state the tentative thesis statement into a full thesis statement for your assignment. The major function of the final thesis statement is to guide your readers to understand your argument that will lead them towards being convinced to believe in it. Consider the following revised tentative thesis into a thesis statement:

1. Thesis Statement of Fact

    - Tentative Thesis Statement: *The use of Internet enables primary school children to cope with the current developments in technology as they grow up.*

    - Final Thesis Statement: *Despite the various challenges, the use of internet services by primary school children in Tanzania helps them to cope with the current challenges of technological advancements as they grow up in this era of globalization.*

2. Thesis Statement of Action

    - Tentative Thesis Statement: *There is a need to provide positive motivation to primary school children in Tanzania to make them use Internet in order to cope with the current developments in technology as they grow up.*

    - Final Thesis Statement: *Despite the existing challenges, there is a need to provide a positive motivation to children at Mbeya city to make them use internet in order to cope with the current developments in technology as they grow up in this era of globalization*

The above thesis statements are different in length. The tentative thesis statement is shorter than the final thesis statement because it is elongated to fit what has been studied in the literature and the experiences of the audience to make it have the features of an effective thesis statement. Kirszner and Mandell suggest that an effective thesis statement has the following characteristics.[37] First, it "clearly communicates your essay's main idea." This means that it communicates the purpose of the whole assignment: the topic and its content.

Second, it "is more than a general subject, a statement of fact,[38] or an announcement of your intent." This means that both thesis statements (that of fact and that of action) are followed by your announcement on what you intend to do in your assignment in defense of that thesis. It means that the thesis statement and your announcement should go together. Consider the following example of statement of fact which is followed by an announcement:

- General subject: *Use of internet services.*
- Tentative Thesis of fact: *The use of internet services is important in the current technological advancements.*
- Thesis statement: *Despite the various challenges, the use of internet services by primary school children in Tanzania helps*

---

37 Kirszner and Mandell, *The Concise Wadsworth Handbook*, 27–28.

38 A fact is different from a opinion. The fact tells what exactly was, is or what is going to happen while an opinion tells about one's own judgment, belief, and feeling about something or situation. Words which show that what one presents is his or her opinion include the following: *I believe..., I suppose ..., I am of the opinion..., I feel..., I think..., I suggest..., according to my judgment...,* etc. Other words are those that show doubt or uncertainty which include the following: *certainly, possibly, likely, often, perhaps, may be, in most cases, sometimes, and usually* (See Wiener & Bezerman, *Basic Reading Skills*, 267–269). These words also show that the statement is your opinion, not fact. It is a statement that one can agree or disagree with it.

them to cope with the current challenges of technological advancements as they grow up.

- Announcement: *In this assignment, I will evaluate the ways in which internet services are used by primary school children in Tanzania in order to cope with the various technological challenges facing them.*

Third, it "is carefully worded." This means that the thesis statement uses simple and direct words avoiding any vague language that may hinder readers from recognizing and understanding it.

Last, it "suggests your essay's direction, emphasis, and scope." This means that the thesis statement suggests the relationship between various ideas in your assignment, the major emphasis, and the arrangement of those ideas in your assignment report. In the above thesis statement, for example, the major emphasis will be put into two main points: "the use of internet services by primary school children" and "the current challenges of technological advancement" caused by globalization which enforce children towards using internet services.

It is easy to arrange the order of discussion within the assignment. The following points may be formulated basing on the thesis statement stated above:

1. The use of internet services among [primary school] children in Tanzania
2. The major challenges posed by the use of internet services among primary school children
3. Internet services to primary school children in Tanzania
4. Current technological advancements and their challenges
5. Primary school children's use of Internet as a coping strategy

Therefore, the effective thesis statement is the one that holds all aspects of your assignment together, directs you in the way to formulate your tentative outline and your writing process, because it highlights all important ideas in your assignment report.

Moreover, the thesis statement, especially that of fact, makes a claim. There are two types of claims, *claims of value or judgment*, and *claims of fact*. Claims of value or judgment are opinions you pose in your thesis statement. Since they are opinions, other people may have other different opinions about them though they have facts in them. This means that other people can debate on the issues made by the claim. They can accept, reject, or provide their own alternatives to the claim made. These are the kind of claims which are mostly expected to appear in thesis statements of students' assignment reports. Consider the following claims of judgment that you can provide in your thesis statement:

1. Chama Cha Mapinduzi (CCM) is the only political party with workable policies in Tanzania.
2. Idi Amini's overthrow was not necessary for the development of Uganda.

Claims of value include statements that individuals or groups of people hold as being true. These are debatable because not all groups of people in the world believe in similar values as being true. Consider the following examples of claims of value you may have in your thesis statement.

1. *Salvation is possible through belief in Jesus Christ only.*
2. *The only way to acquire Nirvana is to follow the eight-fold path.*
3. *There is no god but Allah and Muhammad is Allah's Prophet.*

The above statements are claims of value. They are true only to Christians, Buddhists, and Muslims respectively. They are debatable, and probably unacceptable to people of other religious groups. In this case, claims of value are built upon shared values and assumptions or beliefs; and in most cases, though debatable, they are difficult to support them with concrete objective evidence to convince those who do not believe in them.[39]

Claims of fact are statements; they may be false or true. Since are true or false statements, they are not debatable claims. You

---

39 Howard, *Writing Matters*, 76–77.

cannot debate on a fact; a fact stands as it is. But you can verify this fact. In this case, they are not used in thesis statements which you want to debate on an issue. They are used when you want to verify about an assertion (claim) that cannot be debated on. Consider the following examples of claims of facts that can appear in your thesis statement:

1. *Protein is important for the growth of children* (true statement)
2. *Tanzania got independence in 1948* (false statement)

In whatever claim it contains, a thesis statement is important in arguments because it states your position; it states your perspective or standpoint on a certain issue. It states what you will be defending in your assignment with reasons and evidence; it states the central idea. Hence, a thesis statement "Is a viewpoint, a contention. A good thesis ... is above all *arguable*—that is, not everyone will agree with it."[40] The thesis statement for your assignment report should appear at the end of the first or second paragraph of your introduction part. The advantage for putting it at the end of the second paragraph is that you will have provided a sufficient context when you state it.

Something you should take into account is that not every statement is a thesis statement. The thesis statement has specific components which make it a thesis statement. Susan Anker contends that a thesis statement is composed of two aspects: the *issue* to be argued and *your position* on that issue.[41] Consider the following example of thesis statement of fact:

> *The current minimum salary for teachers is not enough for them to live on.*

In the above example, the issue or subject is the "*minimum salary for teachers*" and the position is "*is not enough for teachers to live on.*" Therefore, in this type, according to Anker, the construction of thesis statement for your argument follows the formula: *Issue/subject + Position = Thesis statement.*

40 Trimble, *Writing with Style*, 21.
41 Anker, *Real Essays with Readings*, 292–293.

However, in some theses, the issue and position are merged together to form a thesis statement. Consider the example of thesis of action below:

- *Standard one should not be forced to stay in the classroom for more that forty minutes.*

Hence, words such as should (not), ought (not), would (not), must (not), etc., can be used to indicate your position on an issue within these types of thesis statements.

Writing the First Draft of Your Assignment Report

As stated in the previous section, the completion of collecting information follows the reformulation of the thesis statement to guide the report writing. Writing an assignment report entails using the re-formulated thesis statement as a guide, and the information you collected in your actual research. You have to use the materials you collected to construct an informed argument to defend your thesis statement, which is the main claim of your assignment. We will discuss about the informed argument in chapter six below.

Writing your assignment report begins with the construction of a logical tentative outline. A tentative outline makes you know which argument you want to make in your assignment, the questions or issues you want to address in that argument, and focus your thoughts without leaving any of them unaddressed. There are three main types of outlines: the *topic outline* which uses phrases in the main and sub-sections of your outline, the *sentence outline* which uses complete sentences, and the *mixed outline* which uses both sentences and phrases in one outline. You have to construct a tentative outline (either topic, sentence, or mixed) with sections and subsections, each supporting the thesis statement in one way or another.

The outline you construct should be logical and focused upon defending or verifying your stated thesis statement. For the outline being logical, it means that the sections and subsections must have a flow that allows your readers to have a glimpse of the sub-arguments in the sections and the way they contribute towards the argument of the whole report. In this case, after reading carefully your collected materials, grouping them into intelligible categories, and understanding what they portray, you have to construct an outline that portrays the whole idea found in the materials. You have to organize the main ideas and small ideas in terms of sections and subsections arranged logically from the beginning to the end.

The outline you construct should not diverge from the main ideas found in the thesis statement because the thesis statement emanates from the collected notes. This means that your outline, though comes from the categories of the collected notes you assembled, it must reflect the main ideas and directives presented in the thesis statement in their order, emphasis and scope. Consider the following example of a tentative topic outline and the way it reflects the main ideas of the stated thesis statement:

A. Topic: *The Use of Internet among Primary School Children at Mbeya City in Tanzania*

B. Thesis Statement: *Despite the various challenges it has, the use of internet services by primary school children in Tanzania helps them to cope with the current challenges of technological advancements as they grow up in this era of globalization.*

C. Main Ideas of the Thesis Statement and their Logical flow:

1. *The use of internet services among children in Tanzania*
2. *The major challenges posed by the children's use of internet services*
3. *Internet services to primary school children in Tanzania*
4. *Current technological advancements and their challenges*
5. *Primary school children's use of internet as a coping strategy*

D. Tentative Topic Outline of the Assignment Report:

1. Introduction
    1. Motivation and Background
    2. Problem and Thesis Statement
    3. Objectives
    4. Methodological Perspectives
    5. Organization and Synopsis
2. Internet Services to Children in Tanzania
    1. Their beginning and Development
    2. Their use to Children and Adults
    3. Their benefits and shortcomings
3. Internet Services to Primary School Children
    1. Primary School Children as a Young Generation
    2. Primary School Children and the Digital World
    3. Primary School Children and the Use of Internet Services at Mbeya City
        1. Positive Effects
        2. Negative Effects
    4. Towards the Future Digital Generation
4. Conclusion

References

The above tentative outline is called *Topical Outline* because it comprises of words and phrases in the form of topics and subtopics arranged in an order to support the thesis statement; it is formulated from main ideas, direction, emphasis and scope of the thesis statement, and written for a particular purpose to a particular audience. It is just tentative because *its role is to just guide you in the process of writing*. This outline is likely to change as you continue with your writing process. The final outline will be obtained when

WRITING YOUR ASSIGNMENT

you have finished all your writing and revising your assignment report. While the tentative outline guides you in your writing process, *the role of the final outline will be to guide your readers (audience) to follow the argument in your assignment report*. Therefore, constructing a tentative outline is one of the challenging stages in your assignment process because it requires you to read your collected notes carefully, arrange your ideas carefully in the way they will appear in your assignment report

You can clearly note above the way the tentative outline reflects the main ideas of the thesis statement and their flow. If there will be no relationship between the outline and the main ideas of the thesis statement, then the report you are trying to write will not defend the thesis statement. Therefore, your report will be directionless and ineffective.

After you have constructed a tentative outline, you have to engage in the writing of the first draft of the report. You have the tentative outline and the collected notes as your primary tools to help you construct a convincing and well-organized argument. Therefore, these two tools are important for you in your thinking and writing process.

You have to not that writing your assignment report is not a mere assembling of notes and evaluating the notes you collected in your actual research process. It is thinking and re-thinking around them and using the new ideas generated from your thinking to produce a constructive argument. This means that the notes you collected will be the *"evidence"* to support what you claim in your sub-arguments in paragraphs and chapters.

Kirszner and Mandell state that "All evidence, however—no matter what kind—must be *accurate, sufficient, representative*, and *relevant*."[42] According to them, the accuracy of the evidence is determined by its source. If the source is *"trustworthy,"* it is likely that the evidence will be accurate. The sufficiency will depend on the amount of materials you will use to support your claims. If you use an adequate amount of evidence, you will have sufficient evidence to support what you claim. Representation is determined

---

42 Kirszner and Mandell, *The Concise Wadsworth Handbook*, 87.

by the range of points and views it presents in regard to the issue dealt with in your assignment report. The evidence should be selected without any bias, representing fairly all different views, both supporting and contradicting, in a considerable range of representation of particular issues. Bias here means your tendency, or a tendency of any other author, "to base conclusions on preconceived ideas rather than on evidence."[43] It is your tendency to select evidence that corresponds to your own views. Relevance depends on the applicability of the evidence to the issue under discussion. It should support what it is supposed to support and not something else. Hence the four aspects outlined above should appear in various ways in your cited evidence because they are the core issues which your readers will use to evaluate the evidence you used in your assignment report.

In most argumentative assignments, as it is in most assignments provided to you by your lecturers, the arguments in their reports will involve assertions (claims) backed up by strong reasons that in turn are supported by evidence. An *assertion* is what you state in regard to your topic of investigation. Evidence is the information you use to support the reasons you stated for the assertion. Evidence can be in the form of examples, statistics and opinions from experts you collected in your notes, excerpts from interviews, observations and questionnaires, photos, and so on. Whatever you assert (claim) should be defended by credible reasons and supported by strong and reliable evidence to convince your readers to believe in what you try to argue for.

However, there are situations where evidence is not necessary. These situations are called *common knowledge* and include the following: self-evident assertions (e.g., when you assert that every creature will ultimately die), equations (e.g., $5 + 5 = 10$), and factual assertions (e.g., Kilimanjaro is the highest mountain in Africa). Therefore, other assertions apart from what is called *common knowledge* require support by evidence.

When writing you are required to evaluate the evidence as you think and re-think about it. You may use the same evaluation

---

43 Ibid., 88.

of the quoted ideas in your notes to evaluate the evidence, reformulate it to suit the argument, or leave the previous evaluation in the notes and re-evaluate it depending on the context of the argument. Therefore, just assembling the collected and organized notes considering them a report is an erroneous endeavor. Remember, collecting and organizing notes into categories, and writing the assignment report using the collected and organized notes are two different tasks in your assignment process.

Conclusion

This chapter devoted to describing the way you can write your assignment, be a research paper or course assignment. It has argued that research is fundamental for producing a well-argued assignment because all claims you make have to be substantiated by evidence. It has pointed out that you can hardly write a convincing assignment report for your readers to believe in what you argue for without evidence. Therefore, strong reasons backed up by reliable, accurate, representative, and sufficient evidence will make your argument convincing to read.

The chapter has also discussed step-by-step the way in which you will move from the assignment question, theme, or idea to writing the first draft of the assignment report. It has provided examples, where possible, to clarify the points made. Therefore, the chapter has built a foundation towards understanding the following chapters.

Chapter Review Questions

1. Define the following concepts as used in this chapter: *writing, research paper, and course assignment*.
2. Discuss the steps to follow when moving from the lecturer's assignment question to assignment topic for investigation.
3. What are the criteria for a good assignment topic you formulate from your lecturer's assignment question?

4. What is the meaning of the term "*literature*"? Explain the important things you have to do when assembling materials for investigation.

5. What is a tentative thesis? Why do you construct a tentative thesis soon after formulating the assignment topic? Clearly explain the terms "*thesis of fact*" and "*thesis of action*" as used in research. With illustrations, differentiate between a *thesis* and a *position*.

6. What is a thesis statement, and why is it important in writing your assignment?

7. What does it mean by the concept of "*reading*" in the process of conducting the actual investigation of the assembled materials? What do you actually do in your *academic reading* of the assembled materials?

8. Discuss the types of sources for your information you have to consult during your investigation.

9. The writing of any research report has to start with a logical tentative outline. Discuss the three types of outlines you learned from this chapter.

10. What does it mean by "*evidence*" in research, and how is it important for your assignment?

Chapter 3

DOCUMENTING SOURCES IN YOUR ASSIGNMENT

Chapter Learning Objectives:

IN THE COURSE OF studying the theme of this chapter, students should be able to:

1. *Define the concept of "documentation" as used in research*
2. *Cite sources in their assignments.*
3. *State the reasons for citing sources in their assignments.*
4. *Use the APA, MLA and CMS documenting styles in writing their assignments*

Introduction

After dealing with the process of writing your assignment in the previous chapter, this chapter concentrates on the way you can document sources in your assignment. The chapter defines the concept of documentation, states the reasons for documenting sources of your information when writing your assignment, states what you should do when documenting sources in your assignment, and briefly discusses some of the documentation styles commonly used by authors in writing academic works. It is expected that at the end of the chapter, you should be well-versed with the fundamental issues of documentation and how to use them in your own work.

What is Documentation?

Richard Bullock and Francine Weinberg state:

> The goal of research project is to study a topic, combining what we learn from sources with our own thinking [to generate new knowledge] and then composing a written text. When we write up the results of a research project, we cite the sources we use, usually by quoting directly, paraphrasing, or summarizing, and we acknowledge those sources, telling readers where the ideas come from. The information we give about sources is called documentation, and we provide it not only to establish our credibility as researchers and writers but also so that our readers, if they wish to, can find the sources themselves.[1] Therefore, documentation is acknowledging the works of other authors or sources of information as you use them in your work using a particular convention or documentation style. It involves your use of references to identify the materials which you relied on when writing your assignment.

Following the above definition, documentation involves the process of providing evidence for what you argue in your assignment or research paper using both primary and secondary sources of your data. Evidence is the fact or testimony that strengthens a claim or conclusion reached in an argument. Documenting sources involves acknowledging other people's ideas that have influenced you in your assignment work or your research to produce a research paper. It means providing credit to the sources of ideas you have cited in your research report.

---

1. Bullock & Weinberg, *The Little Seagull Handbook*, 48.

DOCUMENTING SOURCES IN YOUR ASSIGNMENT

Citing is diligently using other peoples' ideas to support yours, or critique them. In supporting your ideas you use them to strengthen what you argue in your argument. You tell your readers that what you assert is also supported by other sources and not only you. In critiquing the sources you have to do the following: first, assess the *goal* of the author of that source you have cited. Which are the goals of the author? Has the author achieved to reach the planned goals? Second, assess the author's *claims*. What are they? Do they persuade you as a reader? Why are they persuasive or not persuasive? Third, assess the *credibility of the evidence* which the author uses to support the claims. How credible is the evidence used to support the claim. Is it current, relevant, reliable and verifiable? Fourth, assess the author's *argument* in general. Is it sound or unsound argument?

It should always be remembered that someone's ideas are his/her property. They belong to him or her. Documenting sources involves citing honestly all sources used in the assignment paper or research paper and acknowledging (providing credit to) the cited sources using acceptable existing conventions. Strictly speaking, you document when you provide the source of the material you have cited from sources apart from your own thinking to tell your readers that the cited materials are not originally yours.

Why do we Document Sources?

As we have just said, other people's ideas are their property. Since they are their property, they have a commercial value. Therefore, taking and using them in your work as if they are your property is theft. It is not different from stealing a shirt, a trouser, a cup, and so on, from a shop; and if caught, it requires a similar punishment because stealing is an offence by law.

Diana Hacker and Nancy Sommer provide two reasons for citing sources:

- To tell readers where your information comes from—so that they can assess its reliability and, if interested, find and read the original source.

- To give credit to the writers from whom you have borrowed words and ideas.[2]

Hacker and Sommer's above reasons imply that we document sources of information in assignments and research papers to make them thoughtful and well-researched. No authors of books, articles, assignments, or research papers are always perfect in their own thinking alone. Academic writers depend on other academic writers to make their works effective. This means that academic writers build on ideas of other academics in all their works. They can either criticize or support an idea before they build on it. In doing that, the assignment or research paper, becomes well-informed about the current scholarship in regard to the issue being discussed. Writing an assignment or research paper academically means being informed about what other current scholars say on that particular issue and following all required conventions of writing followed by such scholars in your own field of study. Therefore, citing other people's works for the sake of building your arguments on them is inevitable because you have to contextualize your own thinking in the existing knowledge.

Another important reason highlighted by Hacker and Sommer above is that of avoiding plagiarism. Plagiarism is either copying directly, or taking another person's words or ideas as if they are your own. Both directly quoted words and ideas taken from sources should be acknowledged by citing the sources used. Plagiarism is theft; it is cheating readers of your assignment. You must know at this level that any kind of plagiarism in your assignment is totally an unforgivable sin. Documenting sources, honestly and extensively, puts you on a safe side in regard to this kind of literary offence.

---

2. Hacker & Sommer, *The Bedford Handbook*, 689.

DOCUMENTING SOURCES IN YOUR ASSIGNMENT

What do we do when Documenting Sources?

Before documenting sources, we first *cite* and *use* these sources in our own works. What does it mean by *'citing and using a source?'* On the one hand, citing a source is incorporating materials of the source into your own work in the course of your report writing. On the other hand, using a source means making the incorporated materials support what you want to say in one way or another. This means that using sources is citing them, or incorporating them in your text with a special purpose depending on their usefulness and quality. Always the source you cite must help you say properly what you intend your readers should hear. Using a source involves discussing with it; it involves agreeing or disagreeing with the source by providing reasons and evidence for your position. In assignments and research papers, students should '*use*' sources to support what they argue about through discussing the cited source.

The tricky questions which most students have asked are the following: how many times and when should I cite the source or sources to support my argument? Should I cite in every paragraph I write, or every sentence? Should my writing be full of citations to show to readers of my assignment that I have honestly acknowledged the works of other people to avoid cheating? These questions are important to both novices of academic writing and experts alike. Scholars Epstein, Canway and Boden provide us a useful advice:

> It is, of course essential to acknowledge the work of others properly where you have drawn on it. However, it is not necessary to give a list of ten references at every turn of your argument. Such practices are either a sign of low confidence or a way of showing off how much you have read. Note, however, that doctoral theses are a different genre and it may be necessary to reference more heavily to demonstrate that you have done all the reading that your examiners might deem requisite.[3]

---

3. Epstein, Canway & Boden, *Writing for Publication*, 24.

The advice above indicates that there is no single satisfactory answer for the above questions. What you are supposed to do in terms of citing other sources greatly depend on you as author. It does not actually sound good to have the whole of your work full of citations from other writers. Your own words and voice is what your readers would like to hear much, not that of other sources.

There are three main ways you can cite and use sources in your assignment and research paper: Directly quoting sources, paraphrasing, and summarizing.

Directly quoting the source:

Here you quote word for word from the source. Nothing is changed from the original source in this way of quoting. You take everything as it appears in the source you are quoting.[4] However, you are not allowed to quote more than 500 words directly from a particular source without formal permission. You have to ask for formal written permission from the copyright holder of the material and indicate in a footnote that you have been permitted to reprint the materials by using the phrase '*Reprinted with Permission.*' The formal written permission for reprinting materials has to be shown to the research paper or assignment supervisor before submitting it for evaluation. Moreover, extensive quoting of materials from other sources provides to your readers that your assignment is just a collection of other people's works without your substantial input. In this case, as a rule of thumb, "QUOTE texts when the wording is worth repeating, when you want to cite the exact words of a known authority in your topic, when his or her opinions challenge or disagree with those of others, or when the source is one you want to emphasize."[5] Our advice, quote extensively from primary sources and less from secondary sources of your research information.

---

4 Bullock & Wenberg, *The Little Seagull Handbook*, 83.
5 Ibid., 82.

DOCUMENTING SOURCES IN YOUR ASSIGNMENT

Paraphrasing the Source

Here you put the main idea of the source into your own words. In paraphrasing, you do not shorten (condense) the length of the text you are paraphrasing. Instead, you *restate* the main idea of the source in detail in your own *vocabularies, word class* (nouns, adjectives, verbs, adverbs, and so on), *word order,* and *sentence structures* different from that of the source without altering the meaning of the source.[6] Paraphrasing "often means finding plainer, more everyday language, converting passive voice to active voice, breaking a complicated sentence into several shorter sentences, and making the subjects concrete rather than abstract."[7] In doing all these, your paraphrase will automatically be equal to or longer than the original text because what you do is to simplify the more complex text into the everyday simple language.[8]

Kirszner and Mandell provide different features of well written paraphrases as indicated below:

- "Paraphrases are original. They should use your original language and phrasing, not the language and phrasing of the source.
- Paraphrases are accurate. They should precisely reflect both the idea and the emphasis of your source.
- Paraphrases are objective. They should not include your opinions.
- Paraphrases are complete. They should include all the important ideas in your source."[9]

The following guidelines can be useful towards the composition of adequate paraphrases from your sources:

---

6 Ibid., 85–86.
7 Crusius & Channell, *The Aims of Argument*, 37.
8. Ibid.
9 Kirszner and Mandell, *The Concise Wadsworth Handbook*, 381, the bold for emphasis is in original.

- When you write the paraphrase do not look at your source. Read and understand the source; and then, write in your own words what the source says, according to how you have understood it.
- After writing the paraphrase, check it against the source to ensure that there are no repetitions of words from the source. This means that your paraphrase should not have wording and sentence structure closely following that of the original source.
- Make sure to introduce your paraphrase with a signal phrase for your readers to know that you are taking ideas from an outside source.
- Write the page number or numbers of the source which you have paraphrased at the end of your paraphrase. A full documentation of the source should appear in the reference list at the end of your assignment.

However, as a rule of thumb, "PARAPHRASE sources that are not worth quoting but contain details you need to include."[10] Our advice, paraphrase extensively from secondary sources and less from primary sources of your research information. Be sure to enclose in quotation marks all phrases quoted directly from the original source. Consider the following example of paraphrasing:

Paragraph as is in Original

> "From time immemorial, among societies teaching was largely being done as a simple informal activity at home, by parents to their children. This was no exception in African traditional societies. During the golden age of Greece, teaching developed from a simple and informal activity to a most complex and difficult art. By the time African countries were decolonized, teacher training was already formal and systematic. As soon as formal education started in East Africa, preparation of teachers went on simultaneously. There were teachers for bush schools, central schools, and later on junior secondary schools. . . ."[11]

10 Bullock & Wenberg, *The Little Seagull Handbook*, 82, capitalization for emphasis is in original.

11 Mugyenyi, *Aspects of Sociology*, 48.

DOCUMENTING SOURCES IN YOUR ASSIGNMENT

Paragraph as is in a Paraphrase

> Apolo A. Mugyenyi contends that teaching is not a current issue in our today's societies—both in Africa and in the world at large. Even the form of teaching that existed when teaching began does not reflect the form we have today, even in ancient Greece where teaching had a gradual change from "simple to more complex art." However, teaching has been developing from its beginning to the present. In Africa, it has changed from a home-based informal teaching done by parents to a formal complex one. As most African countries gained independence from colonizers, their teaching systems had already developed toward more sophisticated ones. In East Africa, for example, some more developed schools such as "bush schools, central schools, and later on junior secondary schools" were developed. The development of such schools went hand in hand with the preparation of appropriate teachers to teach in these schools.[12]

Summarizing the source

Here you summarize the main ideas of a particular text (source) into your own words and phrases. In summarizing, you shorten (condense) the longer text using your own vocabularies and phrases. You answer the question: *what* does the text say? You try to present what is said by the text concisely and with a clear focus to the point made by the author of the text.

A summary may be shorter or longer depending on the preference of the one summarizing (normally should be one third or one fourth of the text being summarized). In whatever the case, the following are issues to bear in mind while summarizing: use your own words, note key points in the text, note only important ideas among the many presented in the text (avoid concentrating on the details of the text), do note evaluate the content of text, use linking devices to clearly show the relationship between ideas in the text, and arrange the important ideas selected as they appear in

---

12 Ibid.

the original text.[13] Consider the following examples which indicate what you have to do when summarizing:

Example 1: Shorter Summaries

In academic writing, the first sentence of the shorter summary introduces the reader to the name of the author of the text, the title of the text, and then follows the main idea of the text. However, this sequence depends mainly on the documentation style used. The name of the author is mentioned only once in shorter summaries as indicated below.

- *Mligo (2014), in his book* Symbolic Interactionism, *states that . . . (the main idea of the book)(for the APA style)*[14]

Example 2: Longer Summaries

Longer summaries follow the same sequence as are in the shorter summaries. However, the name of the author appears more than once depending on the length of the summary. Normally, the summary uses linking devices to link the ideas of the text summarized as indicated below:

- Mligo (2012), in his book *The Kingdom of God*, discusses . . . (an idea summarized). According to Mligo, . . . (an idea summarized). Furthermore, Mligo notes . . . (an idea summarized) Hence, . . . (conclusion of the idea)

Kirszner and Mandell provide the characteristics of summaries as follows:

- "**Summaries are original.** They should use your own language and phrasing, not the language and phrasing of the source.
- **Summaries are concise.** They should always be much shorter than the original.

---

13 Bullock & Wenberg, *The Little Seagull Handbook*, 87.

14 The American Psychological Association (APA) style of documentation will be discussed in detail in the next section.

- **Summaries are accurate.** They should precisely express the main idea of your source.
- **Summaries are objective.** They should not include your opinions.
- **Summaries are complete.** They should reflect the entire source, not just one part of it."[15]

Consider the example below:

Paragraph as in Original

> "From time immemorial, among societies teaching was largely being done as a simple informal activity at home, by parents to their children. This was no exception in African traditional societies. During the golden age of Greece, teaching developed from a simple and informal activity to a most complex and difficult art. By the time African countries were decolonized, teacher training was already formal and systematic. As soon as formal education started in East Africa, preparation of teachers went on simultaneously. There were teachers for bush schools, central schools, and later on junior secondary schools. . . ."[16]

Paragraph in a Summary

> Teaching has its long history since its beginning. Each part of the world has its own explanation of how teaching evolved and developed. In East Africa, formal teaching went together with the development of teachers. This happened after most countries gained independence. Therefore, in all cases, teaching developed from simple informal form to a more complex one.[17]

There are good and bad summaries. You have to produce a good summary to make your assignment credible and attractive to read. According to Anker, a good summary has four basic aspects you have to consider:

---

15 Kirszner and Mandell, *The Concise Wadsworth Handbook*, 380.
16 Mugyenyi, *Aspects of Sociology*, 48.
17 Ibid.

Writing Effective Course Assignments

1. It has a topic sentence (in a paragraph) or a thesis statement (in an essay) that states what is being summarized and its main idea.
2. It identifies the major support points.
3. It includes any final observations or recommendations made in the original piece.
4. It is written in your own words and presents information [you have understood from the source] without your opinions.[18]

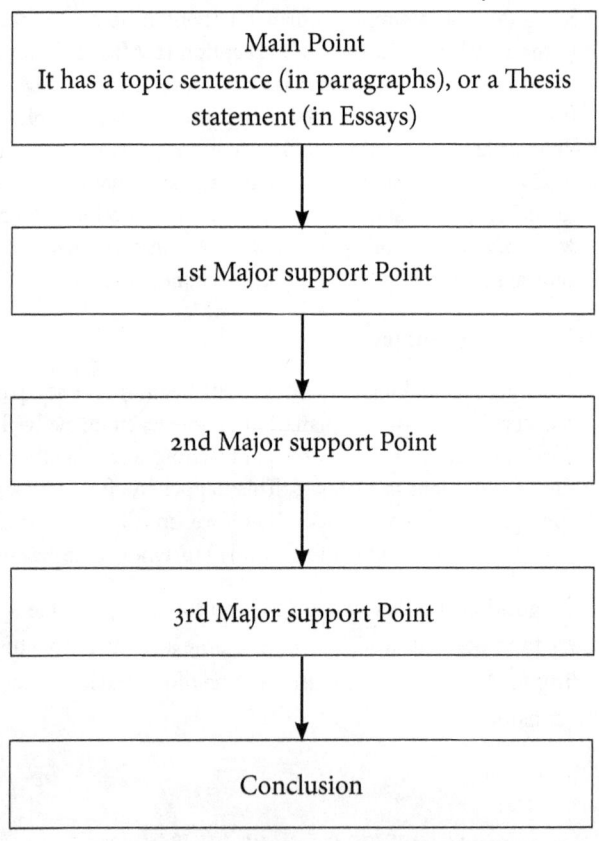

Pictorial View of a summary

---

18 Anker, *Real Essays with Readings*, 279.

DOCUMENTING SOURCES IN YOUR ASSIGNMENT

However, as a rule of thumb, "SUMMARIZE longer passages whose main points are important but whose details are not [required for your assignment]."[19]

Similarities and Differences between Paraphrases and Summaries

The concepts of summarizing and paraphrasing are confusing even to experienced authors. You have to know their similarities and differences in order for you to do justice to them in writing your assignment. One of the major similarities between paraphrasing and summarizing is the use of your own vocabularies and sentence structures (originality) when composing them. To ensure good paraphrasing and summarizing, you have to check for the synonyms of all possible vocabularies used in the original text and construct your own sentence structures. In both of them you do not have to repeat the vocabularies and sentence structures found in the original text. If you do that, you will have committed plagiarism, a serious academic offence. Other similarities include accuracy, objectivity and completeness as stated above.

The difference between a paraphrase and a summary is very slight and sometimes negligible. While paraphrasing does not aim at shortening the text but *restating* it, summarizing aims at shortening the text making it *concise* and to the point. Therefore, a paraphrase can have a corresponding or greater number of words as compared to the original source while a summary contains a rather smaller number of words than the original text.

Summarizing and Paraphrasing involve Understanding What you Read

Writing summaries and paraphrases go together with what you read and understand. Hervey S. Wiener and Charles Bazerman spell it out more clearly: "Most of reading goes on inside your

---

[19] Bullock & Wenberg, *The Little Seagull Handbook*, 82.

head. Your eyes see dark spots on paper, and your brain makes meaning out of those spots and remembers that meaning. This is a lot of activity to keep straight inside your head."[20] The quotation indicates that reading and understanding what you read are both processes. The processes involve underlining, listening and summarizing what you read.

The thing you have to do when you read is underlining or highlighting what you read to indicate the main points of the text. The points can be annotated in your own understanding of what is the main point. The annotations show the list of main points on the margin or within the text. The final stage in the process is to summarize and/or paraphrase what you have understood by expanding the annotated main points.[21]

To summarize this part, the words cited in your work from other sources are called Quotations or Citations. A quotation (citation) can be direct or indirect and its purpose is to provide an example or support a certain claim in an argument. In a direct quotation you quote the words of the source directly. In an indirect quotation you either summarize or paraphrase the idea or ideas of the source. In whatever the case, you have to document (give due credit to) the source. Small directly cited words are normally put in quotation marks to show that they do not belong to the author. Longer quotations are indented from the rest of the text, normally 5 spaces from the left margin. Therefore, documenting the cited ideas is the prerequisite of academic writing. Consider the following examples of direct and indirect quotations (citations) below using the APA documentation style:

Example 1: Indirect citation

> According to Kothari (2002), research as an academic activity involves a scientific investigation about a particular topic of one's choice searching for knowledge (p.1). Kothari's definition of research leads us to considering it as being a scientific,

---

20 Wiener & Bazerman, *Basic Reading Skills*, 315.
21 Ibid., 315–339.

DOCUMENTING SOURCES IN YOUR ASSIGNMENT

systematic, and rigorous activity that demands the researcher's commitment to accomplish it.

The above example comprises of a summarized definition of the source followed by the comment from the researcher on the summarized text. You can note clearly that the author uses different wording and sentence structure from that of the source and uses no quotation marks. However, the author indicates the summarized page for the curious reader to refer to the original source.

Example 2: Shorter direct Citation

> Kothari (2002) defines research "as a scientific and systematic search for pertinent information on a specific topic." (p.1) Kothari's definition leads us to considering research as being a scientific, systematic and rigorous activity.

In the above example, the direct quotation is less than a sentence of the original enclosed in quotation marks (" ") followed by a comment from the researcher on the quoted text. You can note that the author borrows everything from the source: wording, sentence structure, punctuation, etc., and encloses everything borrowed from the source within quotation marks.

Example 3: Longer Direct Citation

Kothari (2002) states thus about research:

> Research in a common parlance refers to a search for knowledge. [One] can also define research as a scientific and systematic search for pertinent information on a specific topic. In fact, research is an art of scientific investigation. . . . Research is, thus, an original contribution to the existing stock of knowledge making for its advancement. (p.1)

Following the above statement, we can say that research is not a mere common place activity. It is scientific, systematic, rigorous and controlled activity.

In the above example, the quotation includes several sentences of the original source, indented five spaces from the left margin, without quotation marks, with a page number where the quotation is taken, and followed by a comment by the researcher on the quoted text. The researcher's comment starts flush from the left margin as it is in the other text.

Types of Citations

After discussing the ways in which you can use in documenting sources in the previous section, this section introduces you to some types of citations mostly used in academic writing. The way to cite is a matter of your choice depending on what you choose to emphasize. You may choose to emphasize on the *information provided by the author* (information prominent citation) or on the *author of the information* (author prominent citation) you have decided to cite. Consider the following examples of citations that use the APA style of documentation:

Example 1: Information Prominent Citation

> *Current investigations on the effects of globalization indicate that most nations, especially African nations are forced to take the bread of their hungry citizens to comply with the debt obligations enforced by the powerful determinants of the globalizing forces (Mligo, 2012: 22).*

Example 2: Author prominent citation

> *According to Mligo (2012:22), current investigations on the effects of globalization indicate that nations, especially African poor nations are forced to take the bread of their hungry citizens to comply with the debt obligations enforced by the powerful determinants of the globalizing forces.*

You can also use *footnotes* or *notes* to document a particular citation whether information or author prominent. A footnote or note is a small number (superscript) placed at the end of the cited material. It is often raised to show difference from the normal text. The footnote number always appears just at the bottom of the same page while the note is always called "*endnote*" and appears at the end of the assignment. The explanation of the item in the cited material bears

DOCUMENTING SOURCES IN YOUR ASSIGNMENT

the same number (at the bottom of the page for footnotes, and at the end of the assignment for endnotes). A footnote or endnote can either be a documentation of a source of information (book, journal article, magazine, and so on), a *content note* providing your elaboration of a point used in the text that could not be incorporated in the text, or both of them. You can see some examples of these aspects in published books and journal articles.

There are three other types of citations you have to know. The first one is *source citation*. In this type, you cite the source of your information. The source here can be an author of a book, journal article, interview, questionnaire, etc. In this citation, the reader expects to see the name of the person or of material where you obtained your information.

The second type is *cross-reference citation* where you cite the same work. In this citation, you refer the reader to another, chapter, page, section, etc., within the same work (your assignment). Cross-referencing is mostly done in order clarify or emphasize a particular point. In cross-referencing we use in the footnotes and endnotes phrases such as the following: for more detail discussion/clarification/emphasis, etc., please see page 6/section 4 part B/figure 5/ footnote 10, etc. Statements like these move the reader to consulting the mentioned part within the assignment in order to have the full elaboration of the idea.

The third type of citation is *explanatory citation*. It is normally called content note because it appears in either footnotes or endnotes. As we pointed out earlier in this section, explanatory citation (or content note) provides additional descriptive explanations about a certain idea within a sentence or paragraph that could not appear in the content of that sentence or paragraph. The explanation could not appear due to space or to being unrelated to what was being discussed in that sentence or paragraph. This citation can either discuss, provide examples, etc. Moreover, it can also add a source of what has been discussed. In this case, we can conclude that the three types of citations can be used in various ways within the text. It can be possible to see all the three types of citations, source, cross-reference and explanatory citations, placed within one footnote or endnote depending on the author's intention.

At the end of every assignment or research paper there must be a list of all the works used in your assignment. The list of works at the end of your report is called *reference list* or *bibliography*. Here, all cited works in your assignment should be listed in full with the author, title, volume, publication data, etc. As we said in the previous chapter when discussion about assembling materials, most students (to their negligence) cite sources but do not include the cited sources in the bibliography or list of cited works. Consequently, they risk subjecting their assignments to suspicion.

What is the difference between a bibliography and a reference list? You have to know the difference between these terminologies to use them correctly in documenting your sources. Reference list or just references is the list of cited works only. That is why it is also called Cited Works. The references or cited works is short and makes easy for the reader(s) to locate the sources they would like to refer to because the list provides only the works cited in your assignment. In contrast, the bibliography includes a good number of materials you have consulted in your search for ideas in the literature (both cited and not cited ones). The bibliography enables your examiners and readers find other interesting materials they would not find in the references list. In that case, bibliography becomes the source of interesting sources for other researchers and authors who deal with a similar problem with yours.

Which are Documenting Styles?

The previous section focused on the types of citations you should use when documenting your sources. This section discusses some documenting styles used in academic writing. It is possible to invent your unique documenting style and use it consistently in your assignment. However, colleges and universities would prefer that you use the already established convention of their choice. There are numerous existing documentation styles or formats that can be

DOCUMENTING SOURCES IN YOUR ASSIGNMENT

used in assignments and research papers depending on the discipline or field of study as categorized in the examples below.

For Social Sciences, the following documentation styles may be used:

1. *Style Manual for Political Science.*
2. *Publication Manual American Psychological Association.*
3. "American Anthropological Association Style Guide"
4. *American Sociological Association Style Guide*

For Natural Sciences and Mathematics, the following style guides may be used:

1. *Scientific Style and Format: The Council of Science Editors Manual of Authors, Editors, and Publishers*
2. *American Chemical Society Style Guide: A Manual for Authors and Editors*
3. *American Medical Association Manual of Style*

For the humanities, the following style guides may be used:

1. *Modern Language Association Handbook for Writers of Research papers*
2. *The Chicago Manual of Style*

What is important is that you have to adhere to the choice of your supervisor or college. If there is no directives from your supervisor and college, select the documenting style that is in your field of study and use it effectively and consistently.

In the following paragraphs we discuss only three of the styles mentioned above: The Modern Language Association (MLA), the American Psychological Association (APA) and the Chicago Manual of Style (CMS).

The Modern Language Association (MLA) Style

This documentation style is mostly used for documentation by authors in the Humanities and Languages. According to the *MLA Handbook for Writers of Research Papers*, 6th Edition, 2003, this style has three parts: parenthetical citation or in-text citation (references made within the text or the body of your assignment), a works cited list, and content notes.

Parenthetical references are in-text citations which appear as short documentations within the text. In this documentation style, the author's surname is placed at the end of the in-text citation followed by a page number both enclosed within the same parentheses. The surname and the page number are separated by a comma. Consider the following examples:

Example 1:

> "Too much passive voices make the paper difficult to understand because it hides the doer of the action, and an excessive use of active voices creates the impression of a selfish author" (Mligo, 56).

Example 2:

> According to Mligo, "Too much passive voices make the paper difficult to understand because it hides the doer of the action, and excessive use of active voices creates the impression of a selfish author" (56).

In the first and second examples above, the period (.) comes after the parentheses to mark the end of the citation. In the second example, a signal phrase is used to mention the surname of the author; the page is placed at the end of the citation being enclosed by the parentheses followed by a period.

The signal phrase is used to introduce directly quoted words, summary, or paraphrase, and may be placed at the beginning, the middle or the end of a sentence/cited content depending on your preferences. Consider the following examples:

DOCUMENTING SOURCES IN YOUR ASSIGNMENT

1. According to Mligo, "Too much passive voices make the paper difficult to understand because it hides the doer of the action, and excessive use of active voices creates the impression of a selfish author" (56). [Signal Phrase at the Beginning of Citation]

2. "Too much passive voices," according to Mligo, "make the paper difficult to understand because it hides the doer of the action, and excessive use of active voices creates the impression of a selfish author" (56). [Signal Phrase at the *Middle of Citation*]

3. "Too much passive voices make the paper difficult to understand because it hides the doer of the action, and excessive use of active voices creates the impression of a selfish author," according to Mligo (56). [Signal Phrase at the *End of Citation*]

You have to use various signal phrases and tenses of verbs according to situation. Avoid using only one or two commonly known verbs or tenses in the signal phrases to avoid monotony. Consider the following examples of how to construct signal phrases to introduce a direct quotation:

1. Mligo (2012) points out that "..."
2. According to Mligo (2012), "..."
3. In the words of Mligo (2012), "..."
4. Mligo (2012) has provided an argument in this view: "..."
5. The analysis of Mligo (2012) showed: "..."
6. "...," Mligo (2012) notes, "..."
7. "...," Mligo (2012) comments.

Verbs such as *admit, contend, agree, report, argue, assert, emphasize, declare, suggest, claim, analyze, believe, note, insist, respond, observe*, etc., may be used according to situation.

As said earlier, when discussing the types of citation above, a content note includes some materials that do not fit smoothly with the content of the sentence or paragraph. They may be definitions of some specific terms, phrases, elaborations, and so on. Content notes appear as footnotes at the bottom of the page or endnotes at the end of the whole work just before the works cited part. The footnote or endnote is denoted by a superscript (a raised number) which bears the first line of that note. The first line of the content note is indented one and a half inches (five spaces) from the left margin while subsequent lines start flush from the left margin. Consider the following examples:

1. In the Assignment Text

    Mligo's illustrations on plagiarism have attracted attention among scholars of research methodology. [1] Some scholars believe that borrowing exact words from other authors without putting them into quotation marks amounts into plagiarism while others do not believe in that.

2. In the Note

    1 Scholars have divided opinions in regard to what entails plagiarism in its real sense. However, the common understanding among them is the notion that one author using the words, ideas or concepts of another person as if they belong to him or her without acknowledging the source (see details in Mligo 63–87.)

The works cited or references are placed at the end of your work, double spaced between lines. The first line in every entry of the references list starts exactly from the beginning of left margin while the following lines are indented one and a half inches (or five spaces) from the left margin. The major components of references are the following:

In Book Entries

 i. Author's Surame, followed by comma (,)
 ii. Author's Surname, first and middle names, followed by a period (.) and one space after a period,
 iii. Book title (main and half titles separated by colon (:)) italicized with all major words capitalized, followed by a period,
 iv. City of publication followed by a colon, and one space after colon,
 v. Publisher (abbreviated) followed by comma (,).

vi. Year of publication followed by a period (.).
Consider the following example:
> Mligo, Elia Shabani. *Writing Academic Papers: A Resource Manual for Beginners in Higher-Learning Institutions and Colleges.* Eugene, OR: Wipf and Stock/Resource, 2012.

Major Components of Article Entries
i. Author's Surname followed by comma (,),
ii. Author's First and Middle names followed by a period (.) and one space after a period.
iii. Article title (main and sub-titles separated by a colon (:)) followed by a period (.). Both main, sub-title and a period are put within quotation marks
iv. Title and sub-title of periodical (separated by colon) italicized, month, year of publication followed by a colon, and pages covered by the article in the periodical.

Consider the following example:
> Mligo, Elia Shabani. "Jesus Christ, a Compassionate Companion: Christological Reflections in the Time of HIV/AIDS." *Acta Theologica.* December 2014: 60–76.

Major Components of Entries from Internet Sites
i. Title of internet site (italicized) followed by period.
ii. Editor of the site
iii. Month and year of last update, followed by period.
iv. Name of institution followed by period
v. Date (day, month, year) of access
vi. Uniform Resource Locator (URL) (enclosed in angle brackets) followed by period.

Consider the following example:
> URT. "Economic Transformation for Human Development." *Tanzania Human Development Report.* Dar es Salaam: 2014. Online at: http://hdr.undp.org/sites/default/files/thdr2014-main.pdf [Accessed 07 September 2016]

The American Psychological Association (APA) Style

APA citation style is mostly used in psychology, sociology, and education. As is the MLA Style, this documentation style also has three main parts: the In-text citation, the Content Note (optional), and the References or Works Cited list. You will be able to document your assignment and avoid plagiarism using these three aspects.

The in-text citation is a short documentation that is done within the text of the assignment report. Since it is short, readers will have to go to the full reference list at the end of the report to view the details of the documented source. In-text citation in the APA style occurs in the following forms:

1. The author's surname and date may appear at the end of the cited content.

Example:

> "Too much passive voices make the paper difficult to understand because it hides the doer of the action, and an excessive use of active voices creates the impression of a selfish author" (Mligo, 2012: 56).

2. The author's surname and date may appear <u>within the</u> signal phrase.

Example:

> According to *Mligo (2012)*, "Too much passive voice makes the paper difficult to understand because it hides the doer of the action, and excessive use of active voices creates the impression of a selfish author" (56).

Or

> According to *Mligo (2012: 56)*, "Too much passive voice makes the paper difficult to understand because it hides the doer of the action, and excessive use of active voice creates the impression of a selfish author."

3. In the block quotation of more than 40 words without a signal phrase but with the name of the author, date and page number appearing at the end of the cited content.

DOCUMENTING SOURCES IN YOUR ASSIGNMENT

Example:

In general, it is agreed among most scholars that:
> Personal interview method requires a person known as the interviewer asking questions generally in a face-to-face contact to the other person or persons. . . .. This sort of interview may be in the form of personal investigation or it may be indirect oral investigation. In the case of direct personal investigation the interviewer has to collect the information personally from the sources concerned. (Kothari, 2004: 97)

4. In the block quotation of more than 40 words with both a signal phrase and the name of the author, date and page number appearing within the signal phrase, or the page number appearing at the end of the cited content.

Example:

> In general, *Kothari (2004: 97)* states: Personal interview method requires a person known as the interviewer asking questions generally in a face-to-face contact to the other person or persons. . . .. This sort of interview may be in the form of personal investigation or it may be indirect oral investigation. In the case of direct personal investigation the interviewer has to collect the information personally from the sources concerned.

Or

> In general, *Kothari (2004)* states: Personal interview method requires a person known as the interviewer asking questions generally in a face-to-face contact to the other person or persons . . .. This sort of interview may be in the form of personal investigation or it may be indirect oral investigation. In the case of direct personal investigation the interviewer has to collect the information personally from the sources concerned. (p. 97)

The signal phrase is used to introduce directly quoted words, summary, or paraphrase, and may be placed at the beginning, the middle or the end of the quoted content depending on your preferences. Consider the following examples:

1. According to Mligo (2012), "Too much passive voice makes the paper difficult to understand because it hides the doer of

the action, and excessive use of active voices creates the impression of a selfish author" (56). *[Beginning of cited content]*

2. "Too much passive voice," according to Mligo (2012), "makes the paper difficult to understand because it hides the doer of the action, and excessive use of active voices creates the impression of a selfish author" (56). *[Middle of cited content]*

3. "Too much passive voice makes the paper difficult to understand because it hides the doer of the action, and excessive use of active voices creates the impression of a selfish author," according to Mligo (2012) (56). *[End of cited content]*

As stated in the MLA style above, a content note in the APA style includes some materials that do not fit smoothly with the content of the assignment. These materials may include definitions of some specific terms or phrases, elaborations that need further attention, and so on. Content notes are placed as footnotes at the bottom of the page; or they may be placed as endnotes at the end of the whole work just before the works cited part of your assignment. The footnote or endnote is denoted by a superscript (a raised number) which bears the first line of that note. The first line of the content note is indented one and a half inches (five spaces) from the left margin while subsequent lines start flush from the left margin. Consider the following examples:

1. In the Assignment Text

    Mligo's illustrations on plagiarism have attracted attention among scholars of research methodology.[1] Some scholars believe that borrowing exact words from other authors without putting them into quotation marks amounts into plagiarism while others do not believe in that.

2. In the Note

    [1] Scholars have divided opinions in regard to what entails plagiarism in its real sense. However, the common understanding among them is the notion that one author using the words, ideas or concepts of another person as if they belong to him or her without acknowledging the source (see details in Mligo, 2012: 63–87).

DOCUMENTING SOURCES IN YOUR ASSIGNMENT

In the APA style, as it is in the MLA style, the works cited or references are placed at the end of your work, double spaced between lines. The first line in every entry of the references list starts exactly from the left margin while the following lines are indented one and a half inches (or five spaces) from the left margin. The entries for references in the APA style are as follows:

A. Major Components of Book Entries

1. Author's surname followed by a comma (.).
2. Initials of the first and middle names both punctuated by periods.
3. Year of publication enclosed in parentheses followed by a period.
4. Title and sub-title of the book separated by colon (both italicized, only the first letters of the first words of the title and sub-title are capitalized, except if it is a proper noun) followed by a period.
5. City of publication (followed by a comma and a state if applicable) followed by a colon.
6. Publisher followed by a period.

The first line is written exactly from the left margin, but the following lines are indented five spaces. Consider the following example:

   Mligo, E.S. (2012). *Writing academic papers: A resource manual for beginners in higher learning institutions and colleges.* Eugene, OR.: Wipf and Stock/Resource.[22]

B. Major Components of Article Entries

1. Author's last name followed by comma (,).
2. Author's initials of first and middle names both punctuated by periods.
3. Year of publication in parentheses followed by a period.

---

[22] This example is only for a book with a single author, without volume number and number of editions. The book with different volumes and editions may have a slightly different way of arranging the entries (Please see APA Style Book for details).

4. Title and sub-title of the article (if applicable) separated by a colon (without quotation marks, only the first letter of the first word of the title and sub-title are capitalized—except if it is a proper noun) followed by a period.

5. The title and sub-title of periodical (if applicable) separated by a colon (both italicized, with the first letter of major words of title and sub-title capitalized) followed by comma, Volume, Issue Number in parentheses (if any), followed by comma, then the page ranges which the article covers within the periodical followed by a period.

The first line of the entry is written exactly from the left margin, but the subsequent lines are indented five spaces from the left margin. Consider the following example:

> Mligo, E.S. (2014). Jesus Christ, a compassionate companion: Christological reflections in the time of HIV/AIDS. *Acta Theologica*, 34 (2), 60–76.

The Chicago Manual of Style (CMS)

This is mostly used in history, fine arts and other humanities except literature. This style uses traditional footnotes and endnotes. To insert a footnote or endnote, you have to place a superscript numeral on the end of your directly quoted or paraphrased materials, or any text you want to document and insert your citation at the corresponding numeral below the page (for footnotes) and at the end of the work (for endnotes). A superscript numeral is a numeral like this ten.[10]

At the bottom of the page, the footnote follows the following conventions:

- It is written single space from one line and another.
- The size of letters is ten font.
- The superscript numeral is indented five spaces from the left margin.

DOCUMENTING SOURCES IN YOUR ASSIGNMENT

- The footnotes and text are separated by a twelve spaces bar line.

Consider the following example of text and footnotes. Endnotes will be arranged in a similar manner at the end of the work.

> Data collection is a process of gathering information from the source in order to answer a particular assignment question. According to Kothari, data a collected as primary and secondary data.[1] Primary data are collected afresh from the source and secondary data are those collected from the secondary source.[2] This means that there are primary and secondary sources of data.[3]

---

[1] See C.R.Kothari, *Research Methodology: Methods and Techniques* (New Delhi: New Age International, 2004), 95.

[2] Aso see Elia Shabani Mligo, *Doing effective Fieldwork: A Textbook for Students of Qualitative Field Research in Higher-Learning Institutions* (Eugene, Oregon: Wipf and Stock/ Resource Publications, 2012), 119—122.

[3] See Mligo, *Doing effective Fieldwork*, 21.

A. Major Components of Book Entries in a List of Works Cited

1. Author's surname followed by a comma (.).
2. First and middle names punctuated by periods.
3. Title and sub-title of the book separated by colon (both italicized, the first letters of the first words of the title and sub-title, and all proper nouns are capitalized, followed by a period.
4. Publication data enclosed in parentheses, i.e., City of publication (followed by a comma and a state if applicable) followed by a colon, Publisher (followed by a comma) and Year of publication. A period is placed outside the parentheses. Consider the following example:

   Mligo, E.S. (2012). *Writing academic papers: A resource manual for beginners in higher learning institutions and colleges.* Eugene, OR.: Wipf and Stock/Resource.[23]

23 This example is only for a book with a single author, without volume number and number of editions. The book with different volumes and editions may have a slightly different way of arranging the required entries (Please see *The Chicago Manual of Styles* Book for details).

B. Major Components in the Article Entries

1. Author's last name followed by comma (,).
2. Author's first and middle names followed by a period.
3. Title and sub-title of the article (if applicable) separated by a colon (with quotation marks, the first letter of the first word of the title and sub-title and all proper nouns are capitalized—followed by a period.
4. The title and sub-title of periodical (if applicable) separated by a colon (both italicized, with the first letter of major words of title and sub-title capitalized) followed by comma, Volume, then year of publication in parentheses, followed by colon, then the page ranges which the article covers within the periodical followed by a period.
5. The first line of the entry is written exactly from the left margin, but the subsequent lines are indented five spaces from the left margin. Consider the following example:

   Mligo, Elia Shabani. "Jesus Christ, a Compassionate Companion: Christological Reflections in the Time of HIV/AIDS." *Acta Theologica*, 34 (2014): 60–76.[24]

The differences between the entries of footnotes/endnotes and those of Works Cited/Bibliographies are listed below:

- Footnotes/endnotes start with a superscript number that correspond to the note number located in the text while the List of Cited Works/Bibliographic entries do not begin with a number.
- The first line of the footnote/Endnote is indented five spaces from the left margin while in the Works Cited/Bibliography the second line and the following lines are indented five spaces.
- Names of the author in footnotes/endnotes are arranged in a normal order (first name, middle, and surname) while in the

---

[24] This example is only for an article with a single author. Articles with several authors may have a slightly different way of arranging the required entries (Please see the *Chicago Manual of Styles* Book for details).

Works Cited/Bibliography the Surname begins, followed by the first name and middle name.

- Commas are used to separate various elements of the entry in footnotes and endnotes while in Works Cited and Bibliography a period is used to separate the elements of the entries.
- In footnotes/endnotes the publication data is enclosed in parenthesis while in works cited/bibliography the publication data is not enclosed in parentheses
- Footnotes/endnotes include page numbers at the end (but does not use abbreviations p. or pp. before the page number) while bibliographical/works cited entries do not include page numbers except for parts of books or articles in journals to show the ranges of pages covered by the article.

Conclusion

In this chapter we devoted a space to discuss the concept of documentation. Four aspects have been the focus of our discussion: the definition of the concept of documentation, how to cite sources, the reasons for citing sources, and the documentation styles. These aspects are also clearly articulated in the writing style guides or documentation style manuals. Each documenting style has its style guide or manual to be used by writers. We can say that a style of writing or style manual is a set of documentation standards to be used by students, researchers and professionals to acknowledge the sources of their ideas as they write their assignments, research papers, journal articles, or books. These styles guide how the way footnotes, innotes, reference lists, and bibliographies should be arranged. They also show the way writers quote and summarize other people's works in their own works. In general, style manuals show how to cite other people's works and how to document those citations.

You should always remember that style manuals in various documenting styles require that book titles, titles of journals, magazines, and newspapers should be *italicized* not underlined.

This is because underlining them may mean that the underlined aspect is a hyperlink to a World Wide Web document. Italicizing differentiates a hyperlink and a title of a document.

Chapter Review Questions

1. What does it mean by the term "documentation"?
2. What exactly are you supposed to do in order to document your sources?
3. State the four guidelines to enable you have an adequate paraphrase of your source. What are the main features of paraphrases and summaries? State the similarities and differences between a paraphrase and a summary.
4. Differentiate between an author and information prominent citation, a footnote and an endnote, a source citation and a cross-reference citation.
5. Mention the documenting styles discussed in this chapter. Select one which you prefer most and discuss how it works for various sources of your assignment.

Chapter 4

USING SOURCES IN WRITING ASSIGNMENTS

Chapter Learning Objectives

IN THE COURSE OF studying the theme of this chapter, students should be able to:

1. Describe the concept of *"using sources"* in the assignment writing process.
2. Read the sources critically as they use them in their assignments.
3. Use integral and non-integral citing strategies in their assignments.
4. Use the various reporting verbs when citing sources.
5. Use ellipses and square brackets in omitting and adding words to a citation respectively.

Introduction

In chapter 3 above, we introduced to you what it means by documentation, what is done when documenting sources, and some styles used in the documentation of sources. We also introduced the concepts of summaries and paraphrasing as used in research report writing. Here some ways of citing sources were discussed and illustrated under summarizing and paraphrasing. This chapter develops the concept of citation of sources further. The chapter starts by explaining what it means by 'using sources' and then discusses the concepts of integral, non-integral citation and reporting verbs, and their roles in the academic writing process. Therefore, at the end of this chapter students should know what it means by using a source and how to use it in their writing process.

What does it mean by Using a Source?

A source of information is a place, a person, or any material which students and researchers consult to acquire information for accomplishing their assignments, or research reports. The source has information that does not belong to the writer (the person writing the report or assignment now); it has information that belongs to the author (the one who wrote the source which the writer consults). Since all academic works should be built on previous academic works, the interaction between the writer and the author is sensitive to produce new knowledge honestly, without jeopardizing any of the present and previous academic works. This is what entails *using a source*. In using a source, the writer engages the ideas of the source to his or her own ideas to produce new ideas. It should be clear here that the author of the source had his or her main idea, which was developed through the incorporation of small ideas, that in turn all supported the main idea.

Using sources is not finding them where they are, copying relevant information, and reporting what you have copied. Strictly speaking, it is not just reporting to your readers the content of the sources and citing the source using the conventionally accepted documenting styles. Using sources also involves your interaction with the sources by reading them critically to understand what they mean, judging their quality in relation to what you argue and stressing their relationship with your argument.

USING SOURCES IN WRITING ASSIGNMENTS

You should be aware that this world is populated by ideas in various forms. However, not all ideas, both written and unwritten, are true and worth of your attention. It is not recommended that you should accept and believe as true whatever thing which someone has just written or spoken without questioning. Faith without questioning is not the nature of the curious mind of humanity. Harvey S. Wiener and Charles Bazerman state: "In some way, you need to evaluate what you read. You need to consider how knowledgeable and trustworthy the writer is and what viewpoints or perspectives the author offers. You should examine how factually accurate the writing is and how trustworthy and based on evidence its opinions are as well as how the authors try to persuade you. Reading well is reading critically."[1]

Using sources involves critical reading, i.e., reading that examines the text beyond what your eyes can see.[2] "To read critically, you analyze the text identifying its main ideas, structure, evidence, or other relevant elements; you evaluate its usefulness or quality; and you relate it to other texts and to your own ideas."[3] At this point, John R. Trimble is right when he says: "A writer eager to improve his [or her] psychological sense never simply reads; he [or she] reads critically. His [or her] mind is always alert to the manner as well as the message, for only in this way will he [or she] learn what works and why it works, plus what doesn't work and why it doesn't."[4]

Critical reading is not criticizing your source in the first place. Though criticizing the sources you read may be involved in the course of your reading, reading critically does not mainly bank on this as its main purpose. It is not criticizing whatever material you read, trying to hammer whatever comes in front of your eyes. Most boastful academics would do that to show that they are knowledgeable about the subject. However, that does not entail what it means by reading critically.

1 Wiener & Bazerman, *Basic Reading Skills*, 307.
2. Aaron, *The Little, Brown Compact Handbook*, 251.
3 Ibid., cf. Aaron, *The Little, Brown Essential Handbook*, 125.
4. Trimble, *Writing with Style*, 7.

As Ann Raimes emphasizes, reading critically "means questioning, discussing and looking at words and images from a number of sides. It also means looking for points of connection and agreement with the writer's views."[5] In order to accomplish this kind of reading you need to develop a questioning mind and an ability to examine the writer's points of views and biases in what they argue and critically examining the evidences they use to justify their claims. It is reading that activates curiosity and enables the generation of new ideas from those presented in the source you read. Therefore, critical reading involves both criticizing and acknowledging of other people's works in order to advance your own work.

When reading critically you do one important thing: *you pose intelligent questions upon the various aspects of the text you read to probe for their credibility.* Raimes[6] suggests that you pose questions on several aspects: first, you pose questions about the author and his or her credentials and reputation in regard to what is presented in the text. Who has written the material you want to read and how credible is this author in the field?[7] You pose questions on the reputation of the publisher of the text. Does the publisher have a careful review system of manuscripts before publication? These aspects will enable you to learn about the purpose of the author and the relevance of the text to its intended audience.

Second, you pose questions to ideas contained in the argument of the text you read. This is done through doubting on the doubtful ideas presented by your author. Do the author's claims supported by credible reasons for claiming? Are the evidences provided credible and strong to support the presented claim or

---

5 Raimes, *Keys for Writers*, 5.

6 Cf. Wiener & Bazerman, *Basic Reading Skills*, 308–309, and Seyler, *Read, Reason, Write*, 34–35.

7 Following this question about the author, you should be suspicious with the credibility of any written materials which have no authors appearing in newspapers and internet despite the value of what they present. This is because you will not be able to evaluate them based on the credibility of the person who wrote them, and no one will be held responsible for what is presented in them should it be proved of having some falsehood.

point of view of the author? Does the author contextualize his or her argument in the context of other similar arguments presented by other authors, or the author presents the arguments by only depending on his or her own knowledge alone without using other sources? This doubting of ideas in the argument will enable you to discern the faulty thinking of the author in the argument. In discerning the faulty thinking you will be able to suggest the better thinking possible.

Third, you pose questions on the logic, consistency, and balance of the argument. Is the argument of the author consistent and logical? If the author uses other people's arguments, how honest is the author in acknowledging them?

Fourth, you pose questions on the way the author uses language in his/her argument. The way the author uses language in the text can either convince you or attract your criticisms. Is the language harsh? Is it discriminating, biased or attractive? Through doubting the language you can discern the possible meaning of the text to the intended audience and to yourself.

At the end of this section we should emphasize that "In college, we don't just ransack sources for information and quotes. *We interact with them.* 'Interact' means both to be critical of sources and to allow them to influence, even change, our point of view."[8] This means that in the writing process, the writer of an assignment can use the main idea of the author of the source or use the small idea in that source that supports the main idea. In whatever case, the writer of the assignment has to have a proper interaction with the ideas of the author of the source in the process of writing establishing a proper dialogue with them. Hence, using a source or interacting with it entails citing and making the source help you (the writer) speak what you want to speak; it entails discussing with the source to bring something new from what is depicted in the source through the critical reading of it.

---

8 Crusius & Channell, *The Aims of Argument* (2003), 207.

Integral and Non-integral Citations

A citation is recognized or introduced to the reader by two ways: a *signal phrase* and *a source*, or by the source only in terms of in-text citation. The in-text citation uses the surname of author, date, and page placed at the end of the citation; or it uses footnotes and endnotes (where a numbered reference directs the reader to a particular numbered note at the bottom of the same page [footnote] and end of the report or assignment [endnotes] respectively).[9] As discussed in the previous chapter, a signal phrase is a phrase that precedes the citation before citing the actual words or ideas of the source. Consider the following examples:

1. Mligo, in his book called *Writing Academic Papers (2012)*, argues: "The academic paper must show clearly the interaction between the author and his/her sources. It does not matter how much evidence the student incorporates in the paper to support the reasons for his/her claim. What matters is the way the student interacts with the ideas, concepts and opinions of those evidences." (p. 52)

2. *Mligo (2012:52)* writes: "The academic paper must show clearly the interaction between the author and his/her sources. It does not matter how much evidence the student incorporates in the paper to support the reasons for his/her claim. What matters is the way the student interacts with the ideas, concepts and opinions of those evidences."

3. *Tanzanian Theologian and Researcher, Elia Shabani Mligo* states: "The academic paper must show clearly the interaction between the author and his/her sources. It does not matter how much evidence the student incorporates in the paper to support the reasons for his/her claim. What matters is the way the student interacts with the ideas, concepts and opinions of those evidences." (p.52)

4. *Research scholar and theologian, Elia Shabani Mligo* believes that any academically written work should indicate clearly the

---

9. Pecorari, *Academic Writing*, 43.

USING SOURCES IN WRITING ASSIGNMENTS

way the writer of the work uses sources in the process of writing. Any academic work that does not show the way the author of the work uses sources looses its credential despite the heavy evidence which the author has used in it (Mligo, 2012: 52).

5. *In his more recent book on academic writing, Mligo (2012:52)* believes that any academically written work should indicate clearly the way the writer of the work uses sources in the process of writing. Any academic work that does not show the way the writer of the work uses sources looses its credential despite the heavy evidence which the author has used.

The words that come before the quotation marks, and before the verb, in examples 1–3 above are called *signal phrase*. This use of signal phrase in citing whereby the name of the author of the source is mentioned as an introduction to the citation that follows is called by linguists an *integral citation*.[10] Integral citations are similar to what we introduced in the previous chapter as *Author Proponent Citations*. In integral citations what follows after the signal phrase is the verb, which is eventually followed by the citation itself. If the citation is actual words of the source, the words are in quotation marks or indented several spaces from the right margin if block quotation. If the citation is a summary or paraphrase of the source (as in examples 4 and 5 above), the verb is followed by words such as *"that," "thus,"* and so on before the exact paraphrase or summary of the source.

The citation can also be recognized without a signal phrase. It can be recognized by seeing the source in terms of in-text citation, footnote or endnote. Consider the following examples for in-text citation:

1. "The academic paper must show clearly the interaction between the author and his/her sources. It does not matter how much evidence the student incorporates in the paper to support the reasons for his/her claim. What matters is the way

---

10. Pecorari, *Academic Writing*, 43.

the student interacts with the ideas, concepts and opinions of those evidences." (Mligo, 2012: 52)

2. It is important to note that any academically written work should indicate clearly the way the writer of the work uses sources in the process of writing. Any academic work that does not show the way the writer of the work uses sources looses its credential despite the heavy evidence which the author has used (Mligo, 2012: 52).

The citation whereby no signal phrase precedes the actual citation is called a *non-integral citation*. It is similar to the *Information Proponent Citation* introduced in the previous chapter. Hence, it means that whether the citation is integral or non-integral it uses in-text, footnote, or endnote citing styles. These are the currently known ways of citing sources.

The Use of Reporting Verbs in Citations

In integral citations, a reporting verb is a verb which shows what the author of the source does in his or her work; doe he or she comment, emphasize, refute, analyze, relate, confirm, assert, note, categorize, discuss, show, measure, concur, compare, account, mention, and so on? On the one hand, integral citations always use reporting verbs that stand between the signal phrase and the citation. On the other hand, non-integral citations do not necessarily require such verbs. They can just be part of the writer's ideas. Consider the following examples of reporting verbs in integral citations:

1. Tanzanian Theologian and Researcher, Elia Shabani Mligo *states*: "The academic paper must show clearly the interaction between the author and his/her sources. It does not matter how much evidence the student incorporates in the paper to support the reasons for his/her claim. What matters is the way the student interacts with the ideas, concepts and opinions of those evidences." (p.52)

2. Research scholar and theologian, Elia Shabani Mligo *believes* that any academically written work should indicate clearly the way the writer of the work uses sources in the process of writing. Any academic work that does not show the way the writer of the work uses sources looses its credential despite the heavy evidence which the author has used (Mligo, 2012: 52).

In the above integral citations (one direct and the other paraphrase) the words "states" and "believes" are "reporting verbs. They stand between the signal phrase that introduces the citation and the actual citation. As stated already, their main function is to tell what the author of the source does in the cited work. In this case, it is important that you (as a writer) use an appropriate reporting verb depending on what the author of the source does in his or her work you cite. In order for you to use an appropriate reporting verb, you have to read and understand the source thoroughly before citing it. There is always a danger for writers, especially because of lack of adequate vocabulary or misunderstanding of the source, to use reporting verbs that are contrary to what the author of the source really does in his or her work. When this happens and recognized, it weakens your work and the author of the cited source.

Roles of Citations in Academic Writing

In the above subsection we discussed the role of reporting verbs in citations. In this subsection we discuss the role of citation as a whole. The role of citation in a paragraph or sentence depends on the way the writer cites the work and his or her intention for citing. Some of these roles are the following:

They show a Confirmation

Most non-integral citations confirm what the writer of the report or assignment knows. In this case, the name of the source is placed at the end of the citation: the summary, paraphrase, or directly quoted words of the source. Consider the following examples used previously:

1. "The academic paper must show clearly the interaction between the author and his/her sources. It does not matter how much evidence the student incorporates in the paper to support the reasons for his/her claim. What matters is the way the student interacts with the ideas, concepts and opinions of those evidences." (Mligo, 2012: 52)

2. It is important to note that any academically written work should indicate clearly the way the writer of the work uses sources in the process of writing. Any academic work that does not show the way the writer of the work uses sources looses its credential despite the heavy evidence which the author has used (Mligo, 2012: 52).

In the above examples, attention is paid to the fact or idea which the source reports. It is not paid to the author of the source. Here the source confirms the idea known widely which the writer knows and uses confidently.

They show the Responsibility of the Author

Citation may be used to show the authority of the author of the source upon a particular idea. In this case, the citation is integral (author proponent) and mentions the author of the source in the beginning of the citing sentence. Consider the following examples:

1. According to Mligo (2012:52), "The academic paper must show clearly the interaction . . . "

2. Basing on Mligo (2012:52), any scholarly written work should indicate vividly . . .

In the above citations the current writer of the work might not clearly know the idea of the source. However, he or she cites it as an authority to what he or she wants to say while putting the whole responsibility to the author of the source. The words such as: *according to, basing on, following, on the bases of,* and so on ascribe the authority about the cited idea to belong to its author.

They show a Common Understanding of the Cited Idea

In some cases, the citation may be used to show that the cited idea is known by both the current writer of the report and the author of the source. Consider the following examples:

1. As Mligo (2012:52) also writes, "The academic paper must show clearly . . . "
2. In a similar way, Mligo (2012:52) asserts that any scholarly written work should indicate vividly . . .

In the above citations, the words *as* and *in a similar way* are comparative words that indicate that the writer also knows the idea he or she cites from the source. Therefore, the current writer shares the knowledge of the ideas with the author of the source. Here, both the current writer and the author of the cited source have equal authority regarding the reported idea.

They show Refutations and Disagreements among Ideas

Ideas are plenty and varied. The same phenomenon, issue or situation may have different ideas produced by different people with different perspectives or points of view. The use of citations in academic writing is one way of bringing together conflicting ideas of different perspectives in order for the current writer of the assignment to discern his or her standpoint or new idea. Consider the following example:

1. Mligo (2011) points out that . . . However, Kinyamagoha (2014) attacks Mligo's claim that . . . To my opinion . . .
2. My own point of view that . . . emerges as a result of an attack of Mligo's (2011) claim that . . . Mligo's claim was attacked

by several scholars such as Kinyamagoha (2014), Mwangosi (2016) and Sule (2015) who argued that . . .

In the first example above, the first part of the first sentence cites the claim made by Mligo about an issue. The second part of the sentence (with "however") indicates the attack of Mligo's claim by another current claim by Kinyamagoha. The second sentence states the standpoint of the current writer who cites the sources basing on the two conflicting sources. There can be two or more sources attacking the same idea (as in example 2 above), or two or more ideas agreeing with the same idea. The stand point of the current writer may be accepting Mligo's idea (attacked by other authors) as being the most convincing about that issue, accepting the ideas proposed by other authors who attacked Mligo, rejecting both Mligo and the other authors and proposing a new one, or accepting all ideas as to be convincing. In whatever the writer does, he or she has to provide strong reasons for doing that. Therefore, through citing ideas from sources, the writers of research papers and course assignments acquire adequate arenas for engaging into discussions with the various ideas about what they write about.

Omissions or Additions in Direct Citations

The previous section discussed the roles of citations in an assignment. This section focuses the attention on the possibility of altering the citation from the original source by either omitting, substituting, or adding information to it. Making a direct quotation from the source does not limit you to whatever presented in the source. You can omit, substitute, or add words and phrases to correspond to the context of your argument. However, such alterations should not affect the general idea of the source. You can omit some words you find unnecessary for your purpose. Consider the following example:

Original Words of the Source

> "Writing an academic paper is a voluntary endeavor. In most cases, the student has to write it in his/her time with his/her own schedule. However, though voluntarily carried out by the student, the student is bound by constraints of deadlines." (Mligo, 2012:63-64)

Revised Source with Omissions when Citing

> "Writing an academic paper is a voluntary endeavor. (. . .). However, though voluntarily carried out by the student, the student is bound by constraints of deadlines" (Mligo, 2012:63-64).

In the above citation, the omitted words are replaced by putting an *ellipsis* (the three spaced periods). The ellipsis indicates that you have omitted a word, words, phrase, sentence or sentences, paragraph or paragraphs within the chapter to contextualize the citation to your argument and the purpose of your citing. Ellipsis may be enclosed in parentheses (as in the above citation) or left without enclosing. In whatever the case, you have to be careful with the punctuations in the source you quote. They should be maintained as they appear in the source.

You can indicate an error in the source by inserting the word [sic] enclosed in square brackets as it appears here. Moreover, you can add words, phrases, or sentences; you can replace a letter or restore the antecedent of a pronoun. In doing all these additions, you use squire brackets to enclose whatever that does not belong to the original source. Consider the following example:

Original Words of the Source

> "The student should not be cheated by the length of materials he/she has presented because the length of materials have little to do with being an effective and convincing piece of work" (Mligo, 2012:28).

Revised Source with Additions when Citing

> "The student [sic] should not be cheated by the length of materials [they have] presented because the length of materials have

little to do with being an effective and convincing piece of work" (Mligo, 2012:28).

Citations can be long or short. Use quotation marks for shorter citations (normally less than four lines) and should be incorporated within the assignment text. Consider the following:

> *According to Mligo (2012:52), "The academic paper must show clearly the interaction between the author and his/her sources. It does not matter how much evidence the student incorporates in the paper to support the reasons for his/her claim."*

If it is longer than four lines, it should be set apart ten spaces from the left margin and not enclosed in quotation marks. Consider the following example:

According to Mligo (2012:52):

> The academic paper must show clearly the interaction between the author and his/her sources. It does not matter how much evidence the student incorporates in the paper to support the reasons for his/her claim. What matters is the way the student interacts with the ideas, concepts and opinions of those evidences.

Conclusion

Writing good research papers and course assignments is not just a miracle. Neither is it a result from a mere simplistic intervention. It involves knowing how to climb on the shoulders of the giants! It involves knowing how to use sources of existing ideas to construct your own. This chapter has in a nut shell just shown you how to do that. It has advocated that using other people's ideas involves an honest knowledge of your role as a writer and the role of the idea of the source to your own work. It is this interaction between you as a writer of the research paper or assignment and the author of the ideas you use which is of interest to any academic who reads your work. It is this academic interaction between you and the sources you use that differentiates your work from a speech delivered by a politician or any other non-academic work. Therefore, you have

USING SOURCES IN WRITING ASSIGNMENTS

to use ideas from other sources honestly and responsibly knowing for sure when to cite, why cite, which to cite, where to cite and how to cite a source in your work. Otherwise, you will cite aimlessly just to increase the number of pages in your assignment, not for academic purposes!

Chapter Review Questions

1. What does it mean by "using a source" to write your assignment?
2. Discuss integral and non-integral citations. What are the components of a citation? Give examples to illustrate your answer.
3. What are the roles of citations in academic work? List them and give examples where necessary.
4. With examples, state the role of an ellipsis (the three-spaced periods) and the square brackets in writing your assignment report.

Chapter 5

ORGANIZING IDEAS IN YOUR ASSIGNMENT

Chapter Learning Objectives

IN THE COURSE OF studying the theme of this chapter, students should be able to:

1. Write well-organized and convincing introductions for their assignments.
2. Write well-unified, well-supported, concise and coherent paragraphs in the body parts of their assignments.
3. Write well-constructed and thoughtful conclusions of their assignments.

Introduction

After grappling with the way you can use sources for writing your assignment in the previous chapter, this chapter discusses the way you should organize ideas in your assignment. The way ideas are presented is an important aspect in academic assignments and research papers. Ideas must be well-presented for easy comprehension of the assignment or research paper. This chapter discusses the

ORGANIZING IDEAS IN YOUR ASSIGNMENT

various parts of an assignment report and how they relate to one another. Normally, a well-presented assignment has three main parts: the *introduction*, the *body*, and *the conclusion*. "In brief, the introduction should establish the problem, the body should present the evidence, and the conclusion should arrive at answers, judgments, proposals, and a closure."[1] Each of these parts should be organized clearly and intelligibly. Therefore, this chapter discusses each part of a well-presented assignment mentioned above to see how it works towards a coherent argument in your assignment report.

The Introduction Part

An introduction is the first part of your assignment report. Usually it serves four main purposes: first, it catches the attention of readers towards reading your assignment in full; second, it suggests or states the main idea which the reader should expect to see in the assignment; third, it provides the background information of the problem you have dealt with it in your whole assignment; and fourth, and most important, it provides your framework (your thesis statement) or the general standpoint which you are for or against throughout your assignment (cf. Arlov 2010: 58) . The attention of readers is captured through arranging the introduction in three main ways: establishing the territory, establishing the niche, and occupying the niche. *Establishing the territory* may be done by putting sentences, questions, an issue, or a puzzle at the very beginning of the introduction. This puzzle or issue must lead you into stating what other writers or researchers have done about that puzzle or issue.[2] Consider the example below where questions are used to draw attention from readers regarding the issue of HIV/AIDS:

- *Why should we bother to remain silent for an issue like this? Why should we not dare to speak as our eyes see people die of HIV/AIDS? These are some of the questions that need us to pay great attention to.*

---

1 Lester D.J & Lester, J., *Writing Research Papers*, 180.
2 Ibid., 180–185.

In establishing the territory, the introduction also may provide the brief description of the main topic to justify the argument or the main idea of the assignment report. This means that the introduction states the background of the issue being discussed and why the discussion of that issue is important. In other words, the introduction states the problem and its background. Consider the following example:

- *The real problem being addressed here is the attack of HIV/AIDS among people at Mtakuja village. This problem has jeopardized the lives of many people, especially youth, since 1981 when it was first officially discovered. We have to address the problem of HIV/AIDS at Mtakuja village because it kills people who are a potential work force of the village leaving orphans without people to take care of. In this case, means to counteract it have to be scrutinized for the betterment of the lives of people in this village.*

Despite the puzzle, questions, or background, you may use an evaluative language in normal statements to emphasize an interesting or important issue related to your study, which will eventually lead you towards introducing what other people have done about it. You can use phrases such as the following to state that issue:

- *One of the central issues in . . . is . . .*
- *It is now generally accepted/recognized that . . .*
- *In recent years, researchers have become increasingly interested in . . .*
- *Recently, researchers have shown an increase of interest in . . .*
- *Many recent studies have focused on . . .*
- *Recently, researchers in many studies have placed much emphasis on . . .*
- *It is easy to note that one of the most important/promising aspects/tasks of . . . is . . .*
- *It may be observed that one of the characteristics/important features of . . . is . . .*

ORGANIZING IDEAS IN YOUR ASSIGNMENT

Establishing the territory is also accompanied by reviewing the literatures to see what other people have done about the issue you discuss in your paper or assignment. Your main focus here is twofold: first, to examine and evaluate what other authors have said in regard to your topic. Second, to establish the relevance of what other authors have said to your own work. In reviewing other people's works, you are expected to follow all documentations as required in citing other people's works. The review of literatures should be critical, analytical, comparative, and argumentative; it should not just be a description, summary, or an annotated bibliography. It also needs to discuss the issues involved with extensive documentation of sources of information while following a clear logic of presentation. Therefore, reviewing literatures is different from mere book reports in the sense that it makes judgments on the worthiness of the source to your work and to the advancement of knowledge in your field instead of just providing a description of the content of the source without reflecting on its value.

Reviewing the literatures is followed by (identification and) stating the gap of knowledge in relation to what others have dealt with. Here you move to the second step of your introduction; you *establish the niche*. This means that you move from the more *general descriptions about the issue* towards *describing the issue itself*. You now specifically state what other writers have not done, a thing you want to do in your paper or assignment. This is done in a more critical way by using the words "however," "despite," "although," and so on. In stating the gap of knowledge you may use the following phrases:

> *Although there has been a considerable amount of research devoted to . . ., researchers have made few attempts in investigating . . .*
>
> *Despite the importance/significance of . . ., authors have paid a little attention to . . .*
>
> *However, few investigations have focused on . . .*

> *However, little research has been undertaken to study the problem relating to . . .*
>
> *However, little is known about . . .*
>
> *None of the published results/findings provide the evidence for . . .*
>
> *No evidence/studies support the . . .*

In order to identify the gap of knowledge, you have to review *relevant* literatures, (i.e., literatures which directly relate to your topic), *authoritative* literatures (i.e., literatures which are published by reputable publishers or reputable journals), and *recent* literatures (i.e., literatures which are currently published or old literatures that still have a considerable influence in your field).

After identifying the gap, indicate the need to deal with that gap. Here you indicate the motivation to deal with the problem or gap you have identified. The following phrases may be useful:

> *The above gap shows that further investigations are needed to ascertain the . . .*
>
> *Until now it remains unclear whether . . .*
>
> *Thus, it would be of interest to us to study/learn/investigate/ . . .*

The third part of the introduction is *occupying the niche*. Here you focus on the exact thing which you want to do regarding the gap you identified. You state the major purpose of your paper or assignment. Your identity must be visible here by the use of the first person pronouns "I" and "We" and the use of the present tense that indicates what you plan to do at that particular moment in regard to the gap you identified. The words: "*This paper . . .*," "*This assignment . . .*," "*This study . . .*," or "*The present work . . .*" are common in this part. The following phrases may be useful for accomplishing this part:

> *In this paper, I discuss . . .*

ORGANIZING IDEAS IN YOUR ASSIGNMENT

In this study, we present the preliminary results of...

In this assignment, we report on...

The major task of this work is to provide...

The paper examines...

The present study analyzes...

The purpose of this paper is to provide...

This assignment report focuses on...

This paper addresses the above questions following the perspective of...

This study expands the model of... to...

This study seeks to understand...

This study is set out to identify...

This study explores...

After stating the purpose of your paper or assignment, you have to state in brief how you will go about filling the gap. The literatures reviewed will normally provide a particular package of knowledge that is related to the topic you deal with in your assignment. This is the available/existing (now known) knowledge about the issue you investigate/study. The gap refers to currently unknown knowledge regarding the topic under the study, which previous researchers did not fill and your study seeks to fill it. It is called *knowledge gap*.

This means that in trying to fill the gap of knowledge you state the method you will use and how you will use it. The method can be a documentary analysis in a library research work, a field work where you will go about interviewing people, and so on. You have to describe each method more widely for your readers to understand, and show WHY you choose the method, however, not so extensively.

According to Pamela Arlov,[3] there are two main types of effective introductions which authors of research reports write to introduce their reports. The first one is what we can call *"broad to narrow"* introduction. In this type of introduction you follow a funnel-like structure. You start the background part with your broad idea and narrow it down to your thesis statement. For short essays, the thesis statement is then followed by the main body. However, for your assignment and other long reports, you can write other parts before the main body depending on the organization of your assignment report.

The second type of introduction is what is called "narrow to broad" introduction whereby you start with the idea which is narrower than your thesis statement. This means that, in this type, your thesis statement is the general statement you have to argue for or against in the course of your assignment writing.

In whatever type, the length of the introduction always ranges from one paragraph to several paragraphs depending on the length of the paper or chapter which you introduce. Remember that in the introduction, you as the author have also to tell the reader what you will discuss in detail in the body of the paper. The author has to tell what the reader should expect to see inside the body of the assignment. The introduction of the chapter should also tell what the reader should expect to see in the body of the chapter. Consider the following example:

- *Following the above stated background, gap and purpose, this paper will concentrate much on the following aspects: the reasons for the vehement spread of HIV/AIDS at Mtakuja village, the reasons for high rates of infection among youth, the need for counteracting the pandemic, and the possible ways through which the pandemic can be counteracted.*

---

3 Arlov, *Wordsmith*, 59–60.

ORGANIZING IDEAS IN YOUR ASSIGNMENT

In whatever way you organize your introduction chapter, it should focus on preparing the way for the argument of your assignment.

The Body Part

The body of the paper follows after the introduction. It is the main part of the assignment where you present the sub-arguments that comprise the main argument of the assignment. It is in the body of the assignment where you report what you discovered from your literature search in regard to your research or assignment question. It is also in this part of the paper where you discuss the findings you discovered in your research by providing your own opinions, quote other people's ideas, and document the evidence from both primary and secondary sources. The presentation and the discussion of the findings may go together, though they are technically different aspects. You have to be as objective as possible in presenting your findings before you discuss them to provide your criticism or opinions about them. This means that presenting the findings is not part and parcel of discussing them. The two aspects are different, and each aspect should be seen clearly in your body part.

The main idea behind presenting the results is showing the evidence you have gathered from the library, or field using the method you stated in the introduction; and the main idea behind the discussion of the findings is commenting and critiquing the presented findings to provide your opinion or stand point about them. You can do both, *presenting* and *discussing* your findings in the same chapter, especially in short research papers and class assignments. In whatever the case, it is important that you pay much attention to the role of each aspect (*presentation* and *discussion* of findings) when dealing with this part in all due diligence. The following phrases may be useful to show how commenting on any piece of evidence (data) you have presented may be done as you begin discussing your findings:

- *The data presented above clarify the relationship between . . . and . . .*

- The data presented indicate/suggest that there is a connection between ... and ...
- The inconsistency of the data presented above is probably a consequence of...
- This particular result may be attributed to the influence of...
- The results above have failed to explain about...
- Although the data presented above shows support for..., mention should be made of some of the limitations of this study.
- The findings of the study presented above have to be treated with certain caution since...
- Notwithstanding their applicability, these findings will still be limited to simply providing advice and guidance.

To write this part well, you should formulate a tentative outline to guide you in the writing process. The body of the assignment report may include several chapters arranged logically according to the logic of the argument being presented. In presenting the argument of the assignment report well, you have to pay great attention to the following aspects: unity, precision, support, and coherence.

Unity

Zinsser William writes: "Unity is the anchor of good writing. It not only keeps the reader from struggling off in all directions; it satisfies his [or her] subconscious need for order and assures him [or her] that all is well at the helm."[4] Unity of the whole assignment has to do with connectivity between thesis statement of the assignment and the supporting chapters. Unity within the chapter has to do with the thesis statement of the chapter and the supporting paragraphs. Unity within the paragraph has to do with the topic sentence that holds the argument of the paragraph while the other sentences support it.

---

4 William, *On Writing Well*, 60.

ORGANIZING IDEAS IN YOUR ASSIGNMENT

Therefore, the unity of your assignment depends on the unity from the paragraph level to the whole assignment report.[5]

In the paragraphs, chapters and the whole assignment, there should be unity of pronouns used, of tenses, of mood or tone, of style selected to use, of attitude portrayed, and of point of view made in the assignment.[6] Most of these aspects are rare even in works of prominent authors in various academic fields! This means that unity has to do with the connectivity of points or ideas in the assignment as a whole. It has to do with the way the ideas in paragraphs or chapters are connected together to form the united whole.

"To ensure that an essay or research paper has unity, make sure that each paragraph is related to your main idea and that all your supporting details in fact support that idea as well as the main idea of paragraph in which they appear."[7] They must be well-organized and clearly stated and should show adherence to one another. This means that they should speak about one and the same thing throughout the assignment.

Precision

Being precise has to do with avoiding unnecessary wording. It purports to enhance simplicity and clarity of what you exactly want to convey to readers of your assignment. William convincingly advises on precision:

> We are a society struggling in unnecessary words, circular constructions, pompous frills and meaningless jargon. . . . But the secret of good writing is to strip every sentence to its cleanest components. Every word that serves no function, every long word that could be a short word, every adverb that carries the same meaning that's in the verb, every passive construction that leaves the reader unsure of who is doing what—these are the thousand and one adulterants that weaken the strength of a sentence.[8]

5 Brandon & Brandon, *Sentences, Paragraphs, and Beyond*, 289.
6 William, *On Writing Well*, 60–62.
7 Blau, Elbow & Killgallon, *The Writer's Craft*, 371.
8 William, On Writing Well, 7.

Support

Here we speak about supporting points that support the main idea (thesis statement) of the whole assignment or chapter in that assignment. Each paragraph must have one point or idea that supports the main idea of the chapter. The point or idea in the paragraph is in turn supported by strong evidence from primary or secondary sources. Normally paragraphs make chapters, which in turn make the whole assignment. This means that in paragraphs is where you will have to include your evidence to back up, validate or establish a justification for what you claim in your thesis statement.[9] It is here where the sub-arguments are constructed. Therefore, if the main points of the paragraph will be supported by weak evidence, chapters will also be supported by weak evidence, and eventually the whole assignment will be supported by weak evidence; and thus, the assignment as a whole will be deemed superficial.

Clarity

Scholar Donald Hall states: "*Clarity* and *coherence* are needed in writing at all levels—from words, to sentences, to paragraphs, to essays, to whole books."[10] Clarity has to do with individual words. You have to play with words in phrases and sentences to select the ones that make your sentence as clear to you and your readers as possible. This means that clarity has to do with your choice of words that effectively make your point—the right words for the right point.[11]

Coherence

While clarity deals with individual words, coherence is concerned about words and ideas and the way they interact to one another.

---

[9] Brandon & Brandon, *Sentences, Paragraphs and Beyond*, 288.

[10] Hall, *Writing Well*, 165.

[11] Ibid.; cf. Williams, *On Writing Well*, 17–43.

ORGANIZING IDEAS IN YOUR ASSIGNMENT

The word *coherence* comes from two Latin words *co* meaning together, and *haerere* meaning to stick. Following the above etymology, coherence means to stick together. Coherence has to do with the method of organization of the assignment and a smooth transition of supporting ideas (evidence) from one idea to another within paragraphs, chapters and the whole assignment. "To achieve coherence, you must present your ideas in a logical sequence—chronologically or spatially; by cause and effect or comparison and contrast; or by order of importance, degree, or familiarity."[12] Hence, coherence has to do with the organization of ideas in your supporting evidence within paragraphs.

An idea contained in a word, phrase or sentence within the paragraph is not coherent when it stands alone; rather, it is coherent when it relates with other ideas within the phrase, sentence or paragraph. Coherence has to do with the way ideas are linked together in a logical flow from one idea to the next.[13]

To make ideas from one paragraph to another coherent, we always use *'transition words.'* Conjunctive adverbs such as however, moreover, as a result, in that case, hence, therefore, similarly, still, then, thereafter, thus, undoubtedly, accordingly, also, anyway, besides, certainly, consequently, finally, furthermore, incidentally, indeed, likewise, instead, meanwhile, next, nevertheless, otherwise, and now are frequently used to connect ideas together. These words indicate that either another idea follows or the present idea reaches an end. Transition words are very important to make the assignment report coherent. Coherence is also achieved through the repetition of key words in sentences and the use of pronouns to refer to the already mentioned antecedent. Therefore, coherence makes your assignment well-integrated, smooth to read, consistent in its arrangement of ideas, and intelligible.[14] Consider the following examples on how to use transition words in sentences within and between paragraphs:

12 Blau, Elbow & Killgallon, *The Writer's Craft*, 371.

13 Hall, *Writing Well*, 165; Brandon & Brandon, *Sentences, Paragraphs, and Beyond*, 288; Williams, *Style: Toward Clarity and Grace*, 81–112.

14 Heineman & Willis, *Writing Term Papers*.

i. **Transitional Words**

Collecting information for research purpose is difficult; *however*, it is worthwhile.

The research problem formulated was not well-focused; *consequently*, the researcher failed to generate adequate research information for analysis.

ii. **Use of pronouns to refer to the previously mentioned antecedent**

Mwendamseke is a good person in the Bena society of Njombe in Tanzania. *He* is praised by every member of *his* village. He owns irish potato farms and engages people to work in *his* farms.

iii. **Repeating key words in a sentence**

It is prestigious to own *a big house* in the village. *The big house* connotes that one is well-off. In this case, *the big house* becomes a sign of one's possession of abundant wealth in the village.

iv. **Sentence Structure**

It is important that sentences be short and clear. However, the precision of a sentence does not depend on its shortness, but on its ability to present only that which it is supposed to present for readers to understand smoothly without or with minimal difficult. Remember, a sentence is always about actors, the action and the one acted upon. The subject of the sentence should show the actor; the verb should show the action, and the predicate the one acted upon. This means that the sentences should be complete with subjects and predicates, not phrases. The use of phrases will hinder readers from understanding the main concept of the paragraph, and of the whole chapter. The use of punctuation marks and capitalization must be correct. Eventually, check for spelling errors.

The main thing to remember in this part of the paper is that you should tell the readers what you intended to tell them, clearly and with all supporting evidence collected to support the answers for the question dealt with within the assignment. Every claim you make must be supported by strong evidence or data from primary and/or secondary sources of research.

ORGANIZING IDEAS IN YOUR ASSIGNMENT
The Conclusion Part

The conclusion of the assignment, chapter, or paragraph is as exciting as the introduction. The main question which the reader of your assignment or chapter will be interested in is probably the following: Does the conclusion made by the the author followfrom what was introduced in the introduction and discussed in the main body of the assignment or chapter? Therefore, an effective conclusion should have at least three aspects: it should follow from the previous discussions of the assignment; it should not introduce something new that was not discussed in the previous discussions; and it should leave the reader with something to think about.

To conclude your assignment, you have to do the following things: First, *summarize, recommend, critique, ask questions, provide advice, or pose a useful assertion on* the main points you have discussed in the main body of the assignment. These are some of the techniques you may use to your assignment. Second, indicate your general stand-points regarding the issue you have discussed, and the *implications* (both theoretical and practical) of the issue you have discussed. Third, state the *way forward*, or what should be done regarding the issues you have discussed, or what future research should be focused regarding the issue you have discussed in your assignment.

In doing all of the above aspects you should not introduce something new. This means that you do not need to bring in something new that was not discussed in the main body of the assignment. Moreover, do not leave the reader asking oneself some questions about anything in your conclusion. Try to make your reader comfortable and satisfied with the ending of the conclusion. Consider the following example of a summary-driven conclusion:

- *In this assignment we have dealt with the main origin of the HIV/AIDS pandemic, the way it spreads, its effects to the Mtakuja youth, and the way to prevent its spread to other uninfected villagers. To my opinion, the problem of HIV/AIDS at Mtakuja village destroys the youth who are the main workforce at the village. The problem still needs attention from both men and women in our society. People of all sectors and professions have to join hands to fight against this horrible pandemic. In doing that, a bright future of the lives of the youth at Mtakuja Village, and the society at large, will be envisaged.*

Conclusion

This chapter has discussed the three major parts of an assignment report: the introduction, the body and the conclusion. It has highlighted the important issues that have to be presented in each part to make it fulfill its purpose. In the introduction you should establish the territory, establish the niche, and occupy the niche. This means that in the introduction you describe what you intend to tell your readers in the body of your assignment.

The body part of the assignment presents the real findings about the topic of assignment. It requires being well-organized with significant unity, coherence, and well-supported arguments. This means that in this part of the assignment you discuss what you promised to tell your readers in the introduction.

The conclusion part should follow from what was presented and discussed in the body part. Here you synthesize what you discussed in the body. It should provide a summary, critique, questions, recommendations or advice on what was presented; it should also show your own standpoints and the way forward. Therefore, a well-presented argument of the assignment merits recognition of the writer and good award of marks.

Chapter Review Questions

1. What does it mean by *"establishing the territory," "establishing the niche,"* and *"occupying the niche"* when writing the introduction part of your assignment? Give examples of each aspect to illustrate your definition.

ORGANIZING IDEAS IN YOUR ASSIGNMENT

2. Explain how the concepts of unity, support, precision, and coherence work in the organization of your ideas when you write the body part of your assignment.

3. What are the roles of transitional words, pronouns, repeated words and phrases in maintaining coherence?

4. What will you have to do in order to conclude your assignment? Explain with a concrete example.

Chapter 6

CONSTRUCTING AN INFORMED ARGUMENT

Chapter Learning Objectives:

IN THE COURSE OF studying the theme of this chapter, students should be able to:

1. Define the concept of "argument" in academic writing.
2. Differentiate between exploratory and persuasive arguments.
3. Identify the main components of an argument.
4. Use the identified components to construct arguments of fact, of action, and of refutation.
5. Construct inductive and deductive arguments in their assignments.
6. Construct well-organized sentences and paragraphs, and know how to incorporate evidence in the arguments of paragraphs.
7. Define the concept of "fallacy" in argumentation, identify the possible fallacies, and avoid them in their arguments.
8. Define the concept of "bias" and avoid biases in their arguments.

CONSTRUCTING AN INFORMED ARGUMENT

Introduction

After discussing the way you can present your ideas with a decent and well-thought introduction, body and conclusion in the previous chapter, this chapter deals with the key issue of presentation—argument. You cannot present any idea, whether in a paragraph, chapter or assignment report, without constructing an argument. The course assignment report must be an informed argument. What is an argument in the first place? This is the first question we have to answer even before we can turn to discussing what it means by informed argument.

The word "argument" comes from the Latin word "*arguere*" which means "*to make clear*." Following this etymology, making an argument is moving "from a vague, private viewpoint to a clearly stated position that we can defend publicly in speech or writing."[1]

Argument in Academic and Non-Academic Arenas

In normal conversations, i.e., in non-academic arenas, an argument means a heated debate between two sides. Each side is said to argue against the other side in regard to the issue under discussion. Usually, this is a polemical and confrontational discussion. This heated discussion is done with the aim of each side winning against the other. In philosophy and logic, academic arenas we are concerned here, argument does not imply debating on the position you are assigned to defend in order to win against the other side. Argument has to do with *making a case*. It means an attempt to convince and persuade someone towards believing in your position through providing *concrete reasons* and *evidence* for accepting the *reached conclusion* about the issue being discussed. It is taking a position or perspective on an issue and defending it with reasons and evidence to support your assertions or opinions about the issue at hand. Hence, it is important that any argument you make in your assignment has the position which you hold (your claim), the

---

1 Crusius & Channell, *The Aims of Argument* (1995), 3.

reasons for holding that position (reasons for making that claim) and the evidence to back up the reasons you have provided.

Therefore, "A good argument is neither a cold exercise in logic nor an attempt to beat others into submission [as it is done in non-academic arenas]. It is a work of negotiation and problem solving in which both writer and reader search for the knowledge that will create common ground between them."[2] It involves "forming and stating an opinion about a debatable issue, gathering and providing support for your idea, organizing logically, expressing yourself reasonably, and acknowledging views different from your own."[3] This means that when you construct an argument, your primary purpose is not to combat, win people, or have the final say about the debated issue as one could expect in non-academic arenas. Rather, your primary goal is to present your position about the debated issue, or the best solution about a particular problem. Normally, a good argument challenges reasonable people to reconsider their own positions about the issue being debated. Hence, a good argument is the one which reasonable people can challenge or acknowledge.

Susan Anker highlights four important points for a good argument as follows:

1. "It takes a strong and definite position on an issue or advises a particular action.
2. It gives good reasons and supporting evidence to defend the position or recommended action.
3. It considers opposing views.
4. It has enthusiasm and energy from start to finish."[4]

Therefore, the main concern of this chapter is to discuss the various ways to achieve the best possible argument that meets Anker's criteria highlighted above. The chapter explores the types of arguments, the main components of an argument, features, fallacies, and ways to avoid bias when arguing your case.

2 Aaron, *The Little, Brown Compact Handbook*, 251; cf. Crusius & Channell, *The Aims of Argument* (2003), 17—18.

3 Aaron, *The Little, Brown Compact Handbook*, 109.

4 Anker, *Real Essays with Readings*, 290.

CONSTRUCTING AN INFORMED ARGUMENT

Types of Arguments

There are several types of arguments. Two of these types are the *persuasive* and *exploratory* arguments. An exploratory argument is *thesis-seeking* or *claim-seeking* argument because in this type of argument your purpose is to consider the evidence you have in order to reach to a more plausible thesis or claim. You first *inquire* about the issue for yourself to determine the truth in it. Your inquiry centers on questions and dialogues with various sources in regard to the preliminary conviction you hold, which eventually leads you upon having your own final standpoint (thesis or claim) on it. Therefore, as Crusius and Channell state that "in the conclusion of your exploratory essay [or argument], you will state a claim whose truth you have tested and earned.... [Y]ou will explore an issue, not make a case for an opinion."[5] The major task in formulating an exploratory argument is to explore about an issue in as detail as possible in order to get the most convenient and plausible standpoint (or thesis) about it.

In contrast, a persuasive argument is *thesis-driven* or *claim-based argument*. Your purpose in this argument is to convince/influence your readers to agree or believe in a certain debatable issue through compelling their feelings and emotions. You show the importance of a particular perspective through logical reasoning and strong evidence to enable readers make sound decisions whether to believe in it or not.[6] "When you write what's usually

---

5 Crusius and Channell, *The Aims of Argument* (2003), 163.

6 Strictly speaking, in academic works such as course assignments, theses, dissertations, research-based books, and journal articles, it becomes difficult to persuade readers. In such audience, you will need to write in order to just convince them to believe in the case you have made. Here, your argument will strive to offer reasons and evidence for your thesis in order to attract their assent. Persuasive argument is mostly used to popular community when working with public issues to influence their emotional stances towards action (e.g., on issues of human rights, on who among the aspirants should people vote, what political or economic situation should the public adapt, etc). In this book I choose to discuss persuasive argument because, as discussed above, one cannot reach it without first formulating the argument for convincing (cf. Crusius & Channell, *The Aims of Argument* (2003), 251–252).

113

called persuasive paper, you pick a controversial issue, tell your readers what side you're, and try to persuade them that you are correct..."[7] Your thesis or claim is the basis for this endeavor.

In a persuasive argument, the main focus is to first *convince* readers to accept your particular conviction about an issue. In convincing, you try to attract the attention and thinking of your readers in such a way that they also hold a similar conviction about the issue as you hold. In order to convince, you have to provide your readers reasons for holding the conviction and evidence to support the reasons you provide. Then, in order to *persuade* your readers, you will have to influence their behavior leading them towards acting according to the conviction. Therefore, the major task of a thesis-driven argument of persuasion is not based on inquiring for the truth of the tentative conviction you hold in order to get the concrete and tested thesis (as the exploratory argument does). Rather its task is to convince other people to hold similar conviction you hold and win their emotional stances influencing them towards acting according to what they have believed on the issue. What you do here is to make a case on an issue and influence your reader' emotions motivating them towards acting.[8] Persuading arguments are centered upon your readers and their interests, prior knowledge, preconceptions, and biases and you have to construct it with the audience in mind.

Both arguments can appear in your assignment as you continue with the writing process. Most report writers start with an exploratory argument in order to get a standpoint or a thesis which is tested and can be asserted with some kind of confidence, and then continue with a persuasive argument where the focus changes towards making a case and influencing readers to believe in it and motivating them to action.[9] In using both arguments it means that you have to earn a standpoint (thesis or opinion) before you can convince and persuade your readers to believe in and act on it.

7 Skwire & Skwire, *Writing with a Thesis*, 1.

8 Crusius & Channell, *The Aims of Argument* (2003), 16—18; Crusius & Channell, *The Aims of Argument* (1995) 3–5.

9. Howard, *Writing Matters*, 75–76.

It means that *exploratory* arguments mostly use inductive logic. The writer cites specific examples, instances or cases from dialogues with various sources as evidence for a general conclusion (claim). Therefore, *inductive* arguments depend on specific examples, cases, or instances you state as premises for the general conclusion. Here you make a case for yourself to believe in. The persuasive argument uses *deductive* logic. It starts with a general statement believed to be true towards a specific conclusion. Here you make a case for your readers to believe in and to be moved to action.[10]

Main Components and Organization of an Argument

As there is a thesis of fact and that of action (see chapter 2 above), there is also an argument of fact and that of action because any argument defends a particular thesis. The two arguments differ in the way they are organized. In the following below, we will borrow examples, with minor modifications, from A. M. Tibbetts and Charlene Tibbetts to show how the fact, action, and refutation arguments are organized in terms of introduction, main body and conclusion:[11]

1. Argument of Fact

    Introduction - Statement of the Problem
                                  Thesis Statement
                                  Definition
    Main Body - *First point* + Reasons + Evidence
                                  Second point + Reasons + Evidence
                                  Third point + Reasons + Evidence
                                  Etc.
                                  Evaluation of points made, reasons and evidence provided.

---

10 Cf. Crusius & Channell, *The Aims of Argument* (2003): 209.
11 Tibbetts & Tibbetts, *Strategies of Rhetoric*, 218–228.

Conclusion	-	Write it to fit the argument provided and the thesis you had

2. Argument of Action

Introduction	-	State the need for action (the problem). State the thesis (the proposed action) Define the terms
Main Body		Give as many fact arguments as necessary Give details of proposed action: expand as necessary. State why and how the action is practical State why and how the action is beneficial State why and how the action is better than other proposed or possible actions.
Conclusion	-	State why and how the proposed action will satisfy the needs introduced at the beginning of your argument.

3. Argument of Refutation

Introduction	-	State errors in your opponent's thesis or main Argument.
Main Body	-	Admit when your opponent's argument is strong (this is both sensible and honest) State flaws in your opponent's argument (arrange the flaws in a graded order, leaving greatest till last). State your own argument of fact or action.
Conclusion	-	Provide a conclusion to fit your argument.

The main components of an argument, whether of fact or of action, are the following:

1. The *thing, idea, issue,* or *event* which the person argues for

CONSTRUCTING AN INFORMED ARGUMENT

2. The *conclusion* reached about that thing, idea, issues, or event—it is also called the *claim* which the person makes.
3. The *premises* which justify the conclusion reached—these are also called the *reasons* why the person reaches to that particular conclusion.
4. The *evidence* to strengthen the reasons provided for the conclusion or claim. The evidence can be in different forms, either data from primary and secondary sources, or examples from real life.
5. The *acknowledgement* of some conclusions not reached or evidence not interpreted and the *response* regarding those unreached conclusions.
6. The *warrants* to justify the relationship between the claim and reasons provided to support it. Warrants are common assumptions about an idea or issue.

Consider the following examples on how to build an *argument of fact* following the above-listed components:

Example 1: The Claim and Its supporting reason

- *Writing a good term paper is always demanding and tiresome (claim) because it requires more energy and time to do it (reason).*

In the above sentence (thesis), the issue you discuss is a term paper and its authorship. You claim that the authorship of a term paper is demanding and tiresome and you support your claim by a reason for it. Remember, a claim is not a fact; it is an assertion drawn from the fact. It is a statement which can be debated and defended to convince other people to believe in what your say. The question of the reader in regard to the above claim would be: *Why do you claim that writing a good term paper is always demanding and tiresome?* The word *"because"* indicates that you now provide a reason for it.

Despite the good reason you provide to support your claim, still readers will question the legitimacy of your reasons. Their question would be the following: *Under which authority do you* convince us to believe in the legitimacy of your reasons? They have to see the evidence to which you base your reasons. Remember, no evidence, no right to speak. The example below shows how you place your reason and evidence when building your argument of fact.

Example 2: The claim, Reasons, and Evidence

- *Writing a good Term Paper is always demanding and tiresome* (claim). *This is because it requires more energy and time to do it* (reason). *A survey conducted by Mligo (2015) among graduate students at the University of Iringa in Tanzania indicates that students had difficulties completing their Course Assignments within the located time despite the greater energy and time they invested in doing them* (evidence).

In the above argument of fact, you have managed to provide an evidence for the reason regarding the claim you made. The evidence is anything that helps to tell your readers that the reasons you gave for your claim are valid ones and worthy believing in. Hence, in the above example, evidence comes from the analyzed data from Mligo's research among graduate students at the University of Iringa in Tanzania in regard to their Term Paper writing processes.

Bear in mind that evidence to support your reasons can be in different forms. According to Aaron evidence you provide to support your reasons can be in one of the following forms:

- Existing facts with a verifiable truth
- Statistical information or facts in the form of numbers.
- Examples relating to the instance being discussed in your assignment.
- Opinions from experts on the subject being discussed in your assignment.
- Beliefs about something known and stated in your claim.[12]

---

12 Aaron, *LB Brief*, 112.

CONSTRUCTING AN INFORMED ARGUMENT

In whatever form you provide, evidence should be accurate (undistorted), relevant (authoritative and current), representative (contextually true), and adequate (sufficient or plentiful enough). The evidence with these qualities is both reliable and convincing to readers of your assignment.

Though you have managed to give a concrete evidence, with all the above qualities, for your asserted reason regarding your claim, yet readers of your argument may still question the reasons you did not provide for your claim, the data you did not consider in interpreting your evidence, or the conclusions you did not manage to state regarding the evidence you have provided. Their question may be the following: *What about that and that which you did not consider in your reasons and evidence?* You have to ascertain their questions before hand and *acknowledge* and *respond* to them. Consider the following example argument with an acknowledgment and response:

- *Writing a good Term Paper is always demanding and tiresome.* (claim) *This is because writing a term paper requires more energy and time* (reason). *A survey conducted by Mligo (2015) among graduate students at the University of Iringa in Tanzania indicates that students had difficulties completing their Course Assignments within the located time despite the greater energy and time they invested in doing them* (evidence). *It is conceivable, of course, that laziness and malingering may cause some of them not to accomplish their Term Papers on time* (acknowledgment); *however, most current researches have agreed with Mligo's findings that students have difficulties in completing their Term Papers despite their maximum efforts* (response).

In the above argument you acknowledge that there is a possibility for laziness and malingering habits of students to be the causes for the failure of students to complete their term papers on time. These two aspects (laziness and malingering) are the possible areas your readers would question about, because you neither considered them in your reasons nor your evidence. You also respond to your readers' assumed question about laziness and malingering.

In acknowledging the possible questions that your readers may ask, you can use one of the following words: *despite, regardless, it is conceivable, notwithstanding, although, even though, while, seem, appear,* and so on. These words show that you acknowledge your readers anticipated question. Then you begin your response with contradicting words such as the following: *but, however, on the other hand,* and so on. These words show that you respond to the readers anticipated question you stated in your acknowledgment stating some possible alternatives. Though it is very difficult to ascertain the question of the reader you do not know, your argument becomes strong if you ascertain it and answer it before hand. Ascertaining and answering readers' questions in arguments is one way of minimizing criticisms from your readers.

Furthermore, you may have a good claim, supported by strong reasons with concrete evidence, yet your readers may see no rationale why they should believe in the reasons you have provided for the claim. Their failure to believe in your reasons for the claim indicates that something lacks despite the concrete evidence you have provided. What is that thing? It is the *warrant*, the principle that shows that the reasons you have given are *relevant* to your claim. Your readers may still ask: Though this reason is factually true, why should it lead us to accept your claim? Here you have to state the principle (the warrant) which shows why you believe that the reason you have given is relevant to your claim. The warrant is a commonplace or generalization which people consider being real and self–evident. Consider the example of the argument with a warrant:

- *Writing a good Term Paper is always demanding and tiresome* (claim). *Few of us can deny that writing scientific work is hard work* (warrant). *This hardness makes students require more energy and time to do it* (reason). *A survey conducted by Mligo (2015) among graduate students at the University of Iringa in Tanzania indicates that students had difficulties completing their course assignments within the located time despite the greater energy and time they invested in doing them* (evidence). *It is conceivable, of course that laziness and malingering may cause*

CONSTRUCTING AN INFORMED ARGUMENT

some of them not accomplish their Term Papers on time (acknowledgment); *however, most current researches have agreed with Mligo's findings that students have difficulties in completing their Term Papers despite their maximum efforts* (response).

The above argument is complete. It has the thing argued for, the claim for that thing, the reason to support the claim, the evidence for which the reason is based, the acknowledgement of possible questions from readers about some unconsidered aspects, its response to reduce possible criticisms, and the warrant to explain why the reason provided is relevant to the claim. Therefore, the seven aspects of an argument are the bases of any simple argument.

For a more complex argument, one claim can have several reasons and each reason being supported by several evidences. The diagram below indicates the more complex argument of fact than the one described above.

Pictorial View of an Argument

Topic Sentence (for a paragraph) or Thesis Statement (for an Essay). It includes your issue and your position

↓

Reason 1

Supported by evidence (e.g., Facts, examples, expert opinions) providing your response to opposing view

↓

Reason 2

Supported by Evidence and has response to opposing views

↓

Reason 3

Supported by Evidence and has response to opposing views

↓

E.t.c

↓

Conclusion

Reminds your readers about your position and makes a strong last attempt to convince towards that position based on the reasons you provided.

Adopted from: Anker, *Real Essays*, 271 with some slight modifications

Consider an example of a more complex argument of fact in one paragraph following the above presented pictorial view:

- *Corporal punishment is not a good way to make students have a decent and acceptable behavior.* (Claim*) Many people and nations in our current time accept this assertion* (warrant). *One important reason for this assertion is that most students*

CONSTRUCTING AN INFORMED ARGUMENT

being punished in that way have continually showed a bad behavior despite the acute punishments they faced. (Reason 1) A good example of this continuing bad behavior despite the punishment is seen in Mtakuja Secondary School whereby 80 percent of students who were corporally punished have either remained with their indecent behavior, or their behavior has been worse than before. (Evidence 1) Despite these results many other investigators have found other useful reasons for the continuing indecent behaviors; nevertheless, their reasons need a separate treatment and consideration. (Acknowledgement and response) Another reason is that corporal punishment hurts students psychologically. (Reason 2) It provides to them a psychological torture that eventually leads them towards seeing life as being meaningless. In a questionnaire distributed to students at Sanjani Secondary School, it was evident that 75 percent of students who were punished with this type of punishment felt no meaning to continue with life after the punishment because the punishment brought to them a sense of shame. (Evidence 2) However, there are some teachers and parents who still consider corporal punishment an important way to maintain decent behavior among students because it makes them contemplate and regret the way they behaved before the punishment. In most cases, these teachers and parents have not adequately weighed good and bad outcomes of the punishment. (Acknowledgement and Response) A better way of punishing students is needed instead of using corporal punishment which hurts more than making students change their indecent behavior. (Conclusion)

In order to move from one reason to another or from one evidence to another you may use transition words such as in addition, one reason, another reason, the first evidence, the second (third, fourth, fifth etc) evidence, most important, in the first place, etc. These words make a smooth transition between one point and another within the argument.

In course assignments, every paragraph, every chapter, and eventually the whole work should present an informed valid argument. This means that the arguments from paragraphs and chapters have to contribute to the main argument of the whole assignment. It means that arguments within paragraphs, chapters, and the whole assignment are very much complex. A claim can have several reasons which in turn become claims supported by other reasons and evidences. The main claim (often called the *thesis*) of your assignment can have several other small claims which are supported by reasons and evidence. What clearly matters is that you have to ensure that your argument is not formed without the incorporation of the above highlighted seven components of an argument in whatever constructions of argument you try to make. Moreover, the argument you make must be well-presented.

Features of a well-presented Argument

Not all arguments have good presentations, nor are they persuasive. For an argument to be well-presented and persuasive, it has to have the following features: first, it should defend a particular side of your interest. This means that it has to take a particular perspective or point of view. However, you have to show readers of your assignment the various perspectives of the idea you argue for before you select one of them to base your argument. This presentation of perspectives demonstrates your knowledge or awareness of the various angles of the argument, and that you have selected to defend that particular perspective for your own important reasons. Hence, you have to select a perspective that you are well acquainted with, familiar with, and that for which you have enough convincing evidence.

The selection of a perspective to guide your study should base on its appropriateness to the issue you want to discuss, its being easy to explain to your readers, and its having self-explanatory power. This means that you have to identify the perspective among the several of them you have just pointed out, state it unambiguously, and explain how it closely relates to your intended assignment. Therefore, your main task here is to make the readers of

CONSTRUCTING AN INFORMED ARGUMENT

your assignment see the important points in your position for them to weigh and decide to agree or disagree with you.

Second, it should be objective. Objectivity is the opposite of subjectivity. Objectivity has to do with being unbiased and not being influenced by one's own emotions or personal prejudices in presenting an issue or issues. If you present a subjective argument, it is likely that your readers will criticize it as being biased, and based upon personal whims and emotions, not on facts and evidences. Most scholars of academic writing discourage the use of first person pronoun (I or We) in presenting an argument to make the argument more objective. In whatever the case, objectivity should be preferred to subjectivity in presenting the arguments of your assignment.

When we say that you should observe objectivity in your argumentation, we direct you to differentiating between the subjective topic and the objective issue you identify from that topic. The topic you select is subjective because it has many issues in it. Each of the issues can be objectively argued for. Therefore, through arguing for an issue identified from the topic with strong evidence to justify the reasons for it, the issue becomes a fact, not a mere opinion, feeling, or belief. Consider the following statement that can make your argument non-objective (biased):

- *Five reasons why* I believe *obesity to be dangerous are* . . .

In the above statement, the words *I believe* indicate a personal bias. They indicate that the reasons for obesity being dangerous are based on just a personal belief, feeling, or opinion. For that case, statements like the one above attract criticisms from your readers of being biased and not based on facts. Instead, you would state it as follows:

- *Five reasons why obesity is considered dangerous are* . . .

Third, the argument should be logical. Logic has to do with the meaningful presentation of ideas in the selected perspective or point of view. As we discussed above, ideas (facts and opinions) are presented in an argument with concrete reasons and convincing evidence. Moreover, there must be a meaningful flow of ideas from one sub-argument to another within paragraphs, one paragraph and another within a chapter, and one chapter and another within the assignment report. You should remember that the argument of your assignment is ONLY ONE; it is made up of several sub-arguments. Hence, the meaningful combination of sub-arguments within paragraphs and chapters is what makes the meaningful argument of your assignment. The inductive and deductive structures of arguments discussed below have good examples of logical arguments.

Inductive and Deductive Structures of arguments

In the previous section we discussed about the argument and its main components. In this section we discuss the two main structures of arguments: the inductive and deductive structures. These two structures are important in reasoning to make it convincing. Therefore, it is expected that when you write your assignment report, you will use one of the two structures, or both of them.

Inductive Argument

In an inductive argument, you start with some specific observations, facts, or your own specific experiences to draw a general conclusion of your argument. This means that you start with specific evidences that support a general assertion about the general phenomenon you argue for. If your readers need a vast amount of evidence before they can believe in your conclusion, this is the argument structure you have to construct. Consider the following examples of inductive argument structures:

- *Mligo studied philosophy to be wise*
  People who study philosophy are wise
  Philosophy makes people wise.

- *Ester married to be happy*
  Married people are happy

CONSTRUCTING AN INFORMED ARGUMENT

Marriage makes people happy

In the above inductive arguments, Mligo and Ester are specific people of your observation. The specific behaviors you observe from them make you generalize to the wider audience. You start from the consequence of philosophy to Mligo (a single person) towards its consequence to all who study it. Again, you start from what marriage makes to Ester, a single specific person, to what it does to all who get married. Therefore, as stated above, inductive reasoning begins with your particular observations of facts to a general conclusion on the applicability of those facts.

There is one thing you have to note in this structure of argument: the conclusion you make is always note certain; it is always uncertain despite the large amount of evidence you may provide to support it before concluding. Why is the conclusion probable despite the amount of evidence provided to support it? It is because you reach it through making inferences. Inference is stating something about the unknown (your conclusion) on the bases of what you know (your specific observations, experiences or facts). However, the more vast and reliable is your evidence to support your general conclusion, the greater will be the possibility for readers to accept this conclusion, and the less probable it will be.

Generally speaking, there is no certainty in this structure of argument in whatever amount of evidence you provide. What you need is to try your best to support it with the most possible convincing evidence. Bear in mind that the fallacy of hasty generalization occurs when you do not supply sufficient amount and reliable evidence to support your conclusion in an inductive argument.

Deductive Argument

A deductive argument is different from the inductive one. While inductive argument begins with specific observations, experiences, or facts towards the general conclusion, deductive argument begins with the general assertion which is believed to be true towards a specific conclusion. In this argument structure, the more important thing is the logic of the argument than the evidence you provide. In this case, readers of this structure of argument will be interested to the syllogism you make.

A syllogism is composed of three-part statements called propositions or statements which present the premises of an issue (the two statements) and the conclusion (the third statement). The first premise of a syllogism is called the *major premise* and is more general statement than the second statement. The second statement is called the *minor premise* and is narrow and more focused. It provides an example drawing from the first more general premise. The third proposition is called conclusion, and is the most specific statement about the issue argued for. Therefore, the three propositions are important in deductive arguments to show how you move from the most general statement you believe to be true and the specific example you draw from your general statement, towards your specific conclusion of your argument. Consider the following example of deductive argument structures:

- *Tall men are handsome (proposition 1)*
  Mligo is tall (proposition 2)
  Mligo is handsome (conclusion)

However, when you talk about a deductive argument having three parts, do not deny the fact that premises can occur in double, triple or more statements, which in sum make more than three statements [conclusion inclusive]. Consider the following example of deductive argument structure with one main statement and several premises:

- *Recent years' writers write good books*–statement/proposition/declaration

Mligo is a writer of the resent years	
This is a resent years' book	Premises
The book is written by Mligo	
This book is good	Conclusion

CONSTRUCTING AN INFORMED ARGUMENT

The deductive argument in your syllogism may be sound or unsound. It will be sound if its true conclusion follows from its true premises, and vice versa. The conclusion of your syllogism must contain everything contained in the two other propositions (the major and minor premises). Therefore, you have to construct good premises in your syllogism to convince your readers to accept the conclusion of your sound argument. If your conclusion will not follow from your true premises, it is obvious that you will have committed a non-sequitur fallacy.

However, the deductive argument may be valid or true. These two words (validity and truth) are different in deductive arguments (syllogisms). The syllogism will be valid if only the conclusion follows from the previously stated premises. In this case, the syllogism may be valid without being true; or it may be both valid and true. Consider the following examples:

Valid Syllogism but not True

- *All white people are liars* (False proposition)
  Anna is a white person (True proposition)
  Anna is a liar. (False conclusion)

- *All cats that are born of human beings lay eggs* (False statement)
  Our cat is born of a human being (False statement)
  Our cat lays eggs (False statement)

In the above example, the first premise (the major premise) generalizes the group of "white people" to be liars. It is true that Anna is a "white person" as the proposition says. Since Anna is one example of white people who are liars, she must also be a liar. Therefore, the truth of one proposition in a syllogism does not make the conclusion of the syllogism to be true. The conclusion in the second part of the deductive argument is valid; however, it is not true because it has false propositions. It is not true that all cats are born of human beings and can lay eggs (first premise); it is also not true that our cat is born of human beings, and cannot be true that our cat lays eggs. Therefore, as you can note, though both of the above arguments are valid (their conclusions follow from premises), they are *not sound arguments* because their claims (conclusions) are not true.

Valid and True Syllogism

- *All mammals have a vertebral column
  Human beings are mammals.
  Human beings have a vertebral column.*

The above syllogism is both true and valid because its conclusion follows from its premises, and all propositions in it are true. In that case, the argument in this syllogism is *sound argument*.

In deductive arguments, it is common to state only one premise (the minor premise) and a conclusion. Consider the following example:

- *Asha is in the list of good workers;
  Therefore, Asha is a good worker.*

The syllogism which misses one of its premises (often the major premise) is called an *enthymeme*. Therefore, the above stated enthymeme could be re-stated with its major premise thus:

- *All people in the list are good workers,
  Asha is in the list of good workers,
  Therefore, Asha is a good worker.*

Therefore, it is expected that you use one or both of the two argument structures discussed above in your assignment to present an informed argument.

Informed Argument

In research activities, especially in research ethics, we talk about *informed consent*. The concept of *informed consent* means that the

CONSTRUCTING AN INFORMED ARGUMENT

researcher has to let his or her informants know about the research, its aim, and the way the researcher will go about it before the informants can participate in the research process. Ethically, the researcher is not allowed to collect data before he or she obtains an informed consent from informants. This means that informed consent has to do with providing information to informants about the research so that they can know it and decide to participate in it or not.

Similarly, the informed argument in an academic assignment has to do with the knowledge and originality of the evidence. You as researcher have to know prior to presentation what the argument is, and organize it in a formal and cohesive way. This means that you have to be informed about the major components of your argument before presenting it. You have to know the main point (claim) of the argument called *thesis* and the small points (claims) of the argument that support the main claim. You have to know the reasons for the claim you made and the original evidence for which to support your reasoning. By original evidence, here it means evidence from data obtained through research. The evidence should not come from your own opinions or emotions. Therefore, presenting an informed argument is crafting the argument from your own knowledge and persuasive ability using original evidence to support the position, claim, or perspective you try to defend.

An informed argument is mostly presented in the form of a well-crafted *essay* which is made of paragraphs and sentences. The link between one paragraph and another is made possible by a concluding statement or a linking device. Let us examine the concepts of paragraphs and sentences more closely.

Paragraphs

A paragraph is a group of logically ordered and interrelated sentences. In academic writing, a paragraph is a container that contains the evidence and reasons for the argument of the paragraph. The good paragraph you construct should have the following qualities:

i. It contains only one point—remember that a paragraph contains only one argument, not two or more. The point which you make in the paragraph is stated clearly in the first sentence called *"topic sentence."* The topic sentence can be placed anywhere within the paragraph. However, it is advisable to place it at the beginning to guide the flow of other sentences in the paragraph. Topic sentences in paragraphs do not normally announce what you want to do, such as: "This paper deals with . . .," This chapter deals with . . .," This paragraph concerns about . . .," etc. A topic sentence that asks questions, that deals with two or more issues, or that announces what you want to do is a weak topic sentence. A strong topic sentence should state the issue specifically and straight, should make one point, and should be possible to verify it.[13]

The main function of a topic sentence is to provide a link between your thesis statement (the general idea of your assignment) and the specific ideas within individual paragraphs. All topic sentences within paragraphs should relate to the general idea of your assignment (your thesis statement) by dealing with a small part of it, or mentioning it in that paragraph. Consider the following example:

Thesis Statement: Despite the various challenges it has, the use of internet services by primary school children in Tanzania helps them to cope with the current challenges of technological advancements as they grow up in this era of globalization.

Topic Sentence 1: Children of this age of globalization grow and develop their minds through the use of internet.

Topic sentence 2: The use of internet posses a lot of challenges to children in almost all places in the world.

Topic Sentence 3: Primary school children in Tanzania should not be prohibited from using internet services.

---

13 Markus, *Write Time, Write Place*, 20–21.

CONSTRUCTING AN INFORMED ARGUMENT

Topic Sentence 4: The current technological advancements are the ones which force children to use internet services in their school activities.

Topic Sentence 5: The era of globalization is irreversible to people of all ages, including children who are in primary schools.

In the above example, each main point of the thesis statement within the five paragraphs makes a topic sentence. It makes its own claim, which is then defended by strong reasons, and supported by credible evidence. One thesis statement in your assignment should produce as many topic sentences as possible depending on the ideas related to it which you want to discuss in individual paragraphs within a particular chapter.

ii. The middle sentences of the paragraph should present the discussion of the topic sentence, or the main point of the paragraph. These sentences present the evidence (data) and the reasons for the point you make in that paragraph.

iii. The end of the paragraph should contain the sub-conclusion and/or the well-placed transition to the next paragraph.

A paragraph may be *transitional, introductory,* or *concluding* paragraph. The *transitional paragraph* connects a section or idea and another within the chapter. It may be a single sentence that allows readers to move to the next point or several sentences that summarize the previous idea before entering to the new one. In most cases, transitional paragraphs do not need topic sentences because they speak about the same idea; however, they need transitional words to show that you move from one point to another in supporting the same idea. .

The Introductory paragraph explains what the reader should expect in the chapter. It states the subject matter as a whole and its component parts. In most cases, the introductory paragraph prepares readers on what follows in the report or chapter.

The *Concluding paragraph* looks back to what has been presented and discussed, and provides the main conclusions and some recommendations (if necessary) about the chapter. Normally, concluding paragraphs do not introduce something new. They stick only to what has been presented, without providing any apologies for it.

You have to keep your paragraphs as short as possible (between 75 and 125 words). Short paragraphs are relatively easier to understand than long paragraphs. You should also keep the variations in the length of the paragraphs. There should be longer and shorter paragraphs to reduce monotony.

Traditionally, a paragraph is indicated trough indentation, or an extra line of blank space separating it from the paragraph below and above if indentation is not done. Indentation is starting a line of the new paragraph far from the margin of the normal line of the paragraph. Normally, indentation is done 5 to 7 spaces from the normal left margin. An indentation shows that a change in the flow of ideas begins. It shows that a new idea follows after the end of the previous idea within the chapter. Therefore, a paragraph is one unit of the cluster of ideas within the chapter. A good example of indentation is the way paragraphs have been organized in this book.

A well-written paragraph has its indicative features. According to Mapungilo, a well-written paragraph should have the following four aspects:

- It should be complete in the sense that it presents the idea or issue fully. The fullness or completeness of the paragraph is achieved when the topic sentence, the supporting sentences, and the concluding sentences are clearly presented within the paragraph.

- It should have unity of what is presented by every sentence in the paragraph. This means that every sentence mentioned above should strictly speak about the idea of that paragraph. Therefore, the unity of sentences makes the unity of paragraphs which make the unity of chapters and eventually the unity of the whole essay.

CONSTRUCTING AN INFORMED ARGUMENT

- Sentences within the paragraph should cohere; this means that they should be arranged in a logical sequence to make the intended point of that paragraph.

- Sentences within the paragraph should have a good chronology. By chronology here it means sentences should sequentially stick to the perspective you select to use in presenting your idea or issue. Are you starting from the general perspective to the specific, or from specific to general? You have to follow a good chronology in whatever perspective you select.[14]

Sentences

As the paragraph is made up of logically ordered and interrelated sentences, the sentence is made up of grammatically and syntactically arranged words and phrases. Strictly speaking, a sentence has two parts: the subject, and the predicate. A subject is not necessarily a doer (agent) of an action; it can only be an instrument, or play a locative role. A predicate is made up of a verb and other syntactic elements like object, adverbial, and complements. Beside, a verb does not necessarily denote action; it can just convey state/condition. Consider the following example:

- Mligo *looks* smart.

A well-constructed sentence in a piece of academic writing should be concise. Concision does not depend on the shortness of the sentence, though necessary. It depends on the necessary words and phrases it has to make its point. A concise sentence has the following aspects:

i. It should be accurate. This means that it should have all the two parts that make up a full sentence—the subject and predicate. Otherwise, it will just be a phrase that can hardly convey the intended meaning.

---

14 Mapungilo, *Communication and Study Skills*, 13.

ii. It should be simple in terms of the words used. In academic writing, simple words are better than flowery words and complicated jargons.

iii. It should be short and to the point. Long and complicated sentences are hard to understand and are in most cases confusing. Keep your sentences short!

iv. It should avoid all unnecessary words and phrases, especially those that do not add more to the required meaning of the sentence.

v. It should be clear without any meandering. If sentences will not be clearly understood, the paragraphs will not, the chapter will not, and eventually the whole work will not either.

vi. It should avoid repetitions of words that will make the sentence complicated.

vii. It should not start with numerals. The number should be written in words and the numeral put in brackets if it is to start a sentence.

viii. It should avoid being sexist. This means that it should be neutral without favoring one sexual orientation.[15]

The following grammatical issues also should be observed when constructing concise sentences in academic writing:

i. Write full sentences with subject and predicate not phrases. Phrases should appear where necessary.

ii. Punctuations should be correct. Check that the full stops, colons, semi-colons, commas, exclamation marks, and so on are placed appropriately in your sentence.

iii. Tenses should be consistent within your sentence except when there is a reason for not being so, e.g., if you are quoting directly from a source.

iv. The subject and verb should agree within sentences. This means that if the subject is singular use singular verb, and

---

15 Cf. Baker, *The Practical Stylist*, 44–57.

CONSTRUCTING AN INFORMED ARGUMENT

if the subject is plural use plural verb. Do not confuse the two within sentences because readers will not understand. Consider the following examples:

- Mligo's *book are* interesting to read (*no subject verb agreement*)
- Mligo's *books are* interesting to read (*there is agreement here*)

v. The sentences should have an appropriate voice. Mostly use active voice than passive voice because active voice helps to explain and understand who performs the action. In the active voice the subject does the action indicated by the verb, but in the passive voice the subject may not even be known. Consider the following examples of active and passive voices:

- *Active voice:* Students read newspapers (*the subject here are the students who perform the action of reading*)
- *Passive voice:* Newspapers were read (*the subject is left out/unknown*)]

The first sentence in the examples above is easier to understand than the second. The question to the reader in the second example will be: Who read the newspapers?

vi. Use pronouns where necessary to avoid repeating the name of the subject that will make it monotonous. However, the pronoun used should agree with the subject. If the subject is plural use a plural pronoun and if it is singular use a singular pronoun. Consider the following example:

- All a*nimals were* placed according to their own categories
  Every *animal was* placed according to its own category

In general, we expect to see a complex argument in your assignment report. A complex argument is composed of many interrelated simple arguments in paragraphs and chapters within the

137

whole report. The following is one possible way of organizing your argument in the assignment report:[16]

1. *Introduction*—here you tell your readers what you are going to tell them: the topic or question of your report, its importance, the purpose of your research, and the main claim of your assignment report (the thesis).

2. *Background Information*—here you tell your readers the context of the claim you stated in the introduction; you state the chronology of events that caused the problem or question you identified.

3. *Reasons and Evidence*—here you provide reasons for the claim you stated in the introduction, and the evidence to support your reasons.

4. *Counterclaim and Counterevidence*—here you refute the issues that are opposed to your own claim which do not convince you and acknowledge the opposing issues that convince you. You can acknowledge the counter claims posed to your claim, yet hold on to your own claim despite the opposing claims and state the worthiness for holding such a claim by providing counterevidence to support it further.

5. *Conclusion*—here you provide a strong and convincing sense of why readers should believe in your claim. You can suggest a solution to the issue you discussed, or a way forward for that issue. You can also put more emphasis on your argument or thesis statement. In whatever the case, your readers must have a sense of your argument as they finish reading. You have to make them think about the main issue as they finish reading your report.

You can easily note that the above form of presentation centers on the main claim of your report. This means that the whole argument of your assignment report will not diverge away from the main claim. Diverging from the main claim will make it be fallacious. We will

---

16 Cf. Howard, *Writing Matters*, 84.

discuss some common fallacies that occur when students construct arguments in their assignment reports in the following section.

Common Fallacies in Argumentation

What is a fallacy? A fallacy is a flaw in your argument. The fallacy indicates that your thinking is not clear, logical and convincing. Fallacies do two main things: they either *evade* the main issue of discussion, or treat the issue *simplistically* by concealing or ignoring the details of the issue. A clear, logical and convincing line of thinking avoids common fallacies in the presentation of an argument.

According to Aaron, fallacies are categorized into two: fallacies due to evasion and fallacies due to oversimplification.[17] We highlight some of the common fallacies in constructing arguments below.

Evasion Fallacies

Ad Hominem

The words *ad hominem* are Latin words which mean "to the person." We say in Latin: "*argumentum ad hominem*" to mean argument to the attack of a person's character rather than the content of the person's argument. This fallacy occurs when you attack the person individually when you argue instead of attacking the issue presented by that person. Remember that when we write, we deal with people's issues, ideas, or arguments not those people who presented the issues personally. Therefore, it is a fallacy to attack the person who presented the argument while avoiding to deal with the argument presented. Consider the following example:

- *John Adam Lusekelo, who is our hospital administrator, is the main causative agent for the ongoing misunderstanding among workers at the hospital. He provides misleading guidelines regarding the working condition of new employees.*

---

17   Aaron, *LB Brief*, 117–119.

In the above example, the issue (*misunderstanding among hospital workers*) is avoided and the author attacks the hospital administrator personally.

Non Sequitur

The word "*non sequitur*" is a Latin word which means "*it does not follow*". This fallacy occurs when your conclusion on a claim does not logically follow from what comes before it. This means that irrelevant evidence is provided to support the claim. Consider the following example:

- Dr. Elia S. Mligo is a good theologian; therefore, he will become a good footballer in our college.

The above argument is fallacious because being a good theologian does not necessarily make someone a good footballer.

Red Herring

This fallacy occurs when your subject matter is destructed and your readers cannot understand the main issue you present. It is hiding a weakness in an argument by drawing attention away from the real issue being argued. Consider the following examples:

Example 1

- Our university college enrolls a good number of students; however, it teaches a good number of subjects.

In the above example, enrolling a good number of students has nothing to do with teaching a large number of subjects. The main subject of argumentation has been destructed for your readers to understand. Are you arguing for the number of subjects taught or the number of students being enrolled at the university college? Here you try to hide the weakness in the enrolment of students (which is the main issue) by directing the attention to another issue of subjects being taught.

CONSTRUCTING AN INFORMED ARGUMENT

Example 2

- Amina: *It is morally unacceptable to walk naked along the road. No one mentally fit has ever intentionally done that.*
  Immanuel: *What is morality by the way?*
  Amina: *Morality has to do with what is considered good by a certain cultural point of view.*
  Immanuel: *Who determines what is considered good?*

In the above discussion, Amina's main issue (walking naked along the road) has been diverged when Immanuel introduced another thing to continue discussing (the issue of morality). This is a fallacy of Red Herring.

Making False Analogy

This fallacy occurs when you do a false comparison. It occurs when you assume that the similarity of things in some ways guarantees the similarity of those things in other ways. Consider the following example:

- *When hungry, people, like dogs, easily get angered and become violent.*

The above example compares people and dogs in terms of hunger and its results. It is true that some people and dogs easily get angered and become violent when hungry. However, it is not all times that all humans and all dogs become easily angered when hungry. To our opinion, the anger of human beings and its effects (violence) cannot be compared to that of dogs in terms of hunger because the two mammals belong to different species.

Bandwagon

This fallacy occurs when you consider something as being true just because you assume that everyone believes it to be true. This is also known as democracy fallacy. It is considering popular ideas to be necessarily right. Consider the following example:

- *Everyone in Tanzania knows that sexual intercourse outside wedlock is sinful.*

The above claim is fallacious because it lacks evidence to support the possibility of all people who live in Tanzania (including children, mentally retarded, Rwandese, Americans, Europeans, and so on.) to hold a similar belief regarding the issue of sex outside wedlock.

Fallacies due to Oversimplification

Hasty Generalization

This fallacy occurs when you do not supply sufficient evidence to support your conclusion about a particular issue you argue for. You make hasty conclusion about a particular issue by considering some few specific issues without considering other variables or factors surrounding the issue. It is also called a *fallacy of insufficient sample, fallacy of illicit generalization* or *fallacy of hasty induction*. Consider the following example:

- *Tanzanian football teams do not do well in international games. Hence, there is no need to support them financially.*

There might be some cases where some Tanzanian teams do not do well in international games. However, what evidence do you have to justify that all Tanzanian football teams do not do well in international games that leads you to the conclusion that they should not be supported financially?

Appeal to Ignorance

This fallacy is called in Latin *Argumentum ad Ignorantiam (argument from ignorance)*. It occurs when you assert that something is true because one cannot prove it to be false. It is an argument for

CONSTRUCTING AN INFORMED ARGUMENT

or against a certain proposition because of lack of evidence for or against it. Consider the following examples:

Example 1:

- *I cannot go to Nigeria, a country where the Boko Haram devastates innocent people. After all, prominent people cannot tell me for sure that I will be safe during my stay there, can they do that?*

In the above example, just because the prominent politicians cannot tell you for sure about your safety, then your claim is true. This is fallacious because your safety in the midst of the devastating Boko Haram group does not depend on the statement or confirmation of the great politicians in that country.

Example 2:

- *I do not know that I am a potential person in the village. Therefore, I am not a potential person in the village.*

In the second example above, since I do not know about my potentiality in the village, I am not potential. It is fallacious because the potentiality of a person in a certain group of people does not depend on the knowledge which that person has about his or her potentiality. People in that group are the ones to determine the potentiality of the person, not the knowledge of the person about oneself.

Appeal to Authority

This argument is called *Argumentum Ad Verecundia* (Argument from modesty). In this fallacy the one arguing does not adhere to the merit of the argument. Instead, he or she attaches the argument to a person of authority to make it credible. It is citing the highly admired or well-known scholar to justify what is being defended in the argument. Consider the following example:

- *Isaac Newton is a great scientist. He believed that the momentum of a travelling vehicle before collision is equal to the momentum it will have when it collides with another vehicle, do you know more than him?*

- *If this idea is good enough to Emil Durkheim who argued a few centuries ago; it is also good enough to me who argue in this century.*

Appeal to the Crowd or Popular Opinion

This is called *ad populum* which means playing to the gallery. Here you claim that a particular idea, opinion, or belief is true because most people believe it to be true. This is an argument where you base on the majority sentiments or popular opinion to support the claim being made in the argument. Consider the following example:

- *Most people in the education sector believe that students' performance increases as teachers reduce providing motivational incentives; so this must be true.*

Circular Reasoning (Circular logic)

This fallacy is called in Latin "*circulus probando*" which means "circle in proving". It occurs when you state or assume a debatable issue or promise as being true. Consider the following example:

- *Investigations on abortions should be prohibited because we cannot acquire something good from such an evil deed.*

The above example is fallacious because it just assumes that abortion is evil and its investigation merits nothing good. However, there is no evidence to support that abortion is something evil.

Sweeping Generalization

This fallacy occurs when you make a general statement that cannot be supported by any amount of evidence you supply. Consider the following example:

CONSTRUCTING AN INFORMED ARGUMENT

- *Every person in Tanzania should be able to read aloud normal computer typed scripts.*

The above statement is an example of a general statement that can hardly be supported by any evidence provided because, obviously, some groups of people, e.g., the blind, cannot read normal computer scripts.

Post Hoc

In Latin length, this fallacy is called *post hoc ergo propter hoc* meaning "after this, therefore because of this". This fallacy occurs when there is no justified link between the cause of the action and its effect. When you state that A causes B, because A comes before B without the provision of sufficient evidence to substantiate that claim, you commit a post hoc fallacy. Since it is true that the cause precedes the effect, it is not necessarily true that all precedence should cause the effect. Consider the following example:

- *Ambindwile, one of the staff members at Tumaini University Makumira Mbeya Centre in Tanzania, wrote many books on research. This must be the reason for many lecturers at Mbeya Centre to develop interests in doing research.*

In the above example, the provider of the argument is sure that just because Ambindwile writes books; it is the cause for the interest of lecturers at Mbeya Centre towards conducting research. However, this is not necessarily the only factor that stirs lecturers to develop interest in research at Mbeya Centre. Here the evidence provided fails to justify the claim. You need some evidence to convince people to believe that there is a link between Ambindwile's writing of books and the interest of lecturers towards conducting research.

The either /or Fallacy

This fallacy occurs when you state that unless a particular issue is done, then some thing will not be successful. This means that the success of a particular thing depends on doing something. It is sometimes known as bifurcation or false dilemma whereby the two categories argued are exclusive and exhaustive. In this fallacy the category becomes a member of one or the other group, not of both. Consider the following examples:

- Either we establish a dispensary at our college, or all students living in the hostel will die of malaria.
- Either you favor Idi Amini's policies and live, or reject them and die.

The first statement above is fallacious because the prevention of the death of students due to malaria does not depend only on the establishment of a dispensary. You may establish a good dispensary, yet students die of malaria. The statement does not consider the other possible factors for the death of students apart from malaria.

Avoiding Bias in your Argumentation

After discussing the main fallacies in argumentation in the previous section, this section discusses the ways you can avoid them in your argumentation. You may avoid all the above highlighted fallacies and present a sound deductive argument, or a well substantiated inductive argument, but still the argument remains biased. You have to avoid all kinds of biases to be blameless. What is a bias? A bias is just a habit of considering some ideas or assertions as being the most correct and worthy of utmost attention as compared to others; it is a habit you develop in the course of your study, interaction, or writing. You will be biased if the conclusions or assertions you make will not be based on evidence, but on your own premature ideas or opinions. This means that conclusions based on what you just want to see or evidence that support your own standpoint without considering other point of views will be a clear indication that you are biased.

Some of the indications of bias include, but not limited to, the following: first, the way you use evidence in your writing process.

CONSTRUCTING AN INFORMED ARGUMENT

If you will select examples, statistics, and so on, that support your position only, you will be biased. Evidence selected should be balanced. You should use evidence that support and that which contradict your position to be fair in arguing your case.

Second, the use of sexist or racist language in your argument is a clear indication of your bias. If you assume in your writing that a certain gender has more ability in a particular issue than another, then you are biased. For example, an assumption that females are weaker in Mathematics than males; or males are weaker in cookery related subjects than females, indicate a biased assumption. An assumption that the black race has a link with poverty is also a biased assumption. The language you use in writing your assignment should be balanced, without bias.

Third, the tone of your assignment report (the whole or part of it) can indicate a bias through the attitude it portrays. When you write, your emotional stance is portrayed within the written script. The emotional stance, therefore, indicates your bias. For example, when you write your report while angry, your anger will be denoted in the report. The anger within the report can make the reader sense your unfair treatment of the subject in your argument because of the portrayed emotional bias caused by anger. It is advisable that the tone you use in your assignment report be balanced, without biases. This will be possible only when you control your mood while writing avoiding portraying your emotional stance within your report.

Fourth, the way you state the things you consider to be important may indicate a bias. If you clearly declare that you believe in something more than the other, that statement indicates your bias. For example, if you state that you believe strongly that children have little contribution in the national development, that statement indicates your bias. You have to be as neutral as possible; otherwise, you have to provide strong evidence to support your claim. Remember that bias appears when you fail to provide strongly convincing evidence to support your claims but base your conclusions on mere premature ideas or opinions.

Fifth, biases will also be noted in the way you select experts to cite in the report of your assignment. If you select experts with only a particular opinion, especially those who only support your own standpoints, or only those who oppose a particular standpoint, you will be biased. You should cite experts with a wide range of opinions to enhance a fair discussion of a particular subject matter.

Conclusion

This chapter dealt specifically with the argument which is the key issue involved in presenting ideas in your assignment. It has shown that the assignment writers will be able to convince and persuade their readers through concrete reasons and evidence for a certain conclusion (thesis statement) they provide. This is what this chapter has referred to as an argument.

An argument is a tool employed to present your main and supporting ideas in writing your assignment. Since the argument convinces and persuades readers to accept your idea, the argument should be built and supported with concrete reasons and evidence to draw convincing conclusions based on the established thesis statement guiding the assignment. In this case, a valid and sound argument should be comprised of important components, namely *the thing being argued, the true conclusion proposed, the true premises or reasons, the evidence to support the reasons, the acknowledgements* and *the warrants.*

It has been evident in this chapter that in the academic writing, in which you write your assignment, arguments occur in two categories, the *inductive* and *deductive* argument. In inductive argument you flow your ideas from specific to general ideas, while in the deductive argument you break the general idea to specific idea. Something important to note is that the well informed arguments you present in your assignment or paper are organized in chapters, which are made up of different paragraphs, which also, in turn comprise of different sentences. Developing an argument requires you as a writer to maintain concision; otherwise, fallacious arguments will be developed leading to your assignment being

CONSTRUCTING AN INFORMED ARGUMENT

weak. Usually, authors of different assignments commit fallacies because of making false analogy, assuming that something is true because everyone believes it to be true, making hasty generalizations, appealing to ignorance, circular reasoning, overgeneralization without supporting evidence, lack of justified link between the cause and its effect, and assuming that occurrence of one event determines occurrence of the other. While trying to avoid fallacies in argumentation, it is also important to get rid of your biases in constructing sound arguments in your assignment.

The final note: After you have completed your argument or your assignment please *edit* and *revise* it from the beginning to the end. In editing, you correct mistakes in spellings, punctuations, and capitalization. You have to cut, change or add words and phrases in the sentence (not the whole sentence or paragraph). In revising, you have to work with the contents, organizations, the effectiveness of language used in paragraphs, chapters and the assignment as a whole. Pamela Arlov states the etymology of the world revise from which we draw of what you are supposed to do when you do the revising. She says: "The word *revise* combines the Latin root meaning *to see* with the prefix meaning again . . . [Hence] to revise is *to see again*, and seeing again is exactly what you need to do as you revise."[18]

You have to sharpen ideas in the paragraph, section, subsection, chapter or the whole assignment to make them stronger. In the revising process you can change words, add sentences or paragraphs, remove sentences or paragraphs, add or remove chapter in order to make your assignment idea or ideas in paragraphs, and chapters clear and convincing. Arlov suggests that in order for you to be able to see your assignment report again, "you need to create a mental distance between yourself and the work. You can best achieve this mental distance with time. Lay the writing aside for at least twenty-four hours. When you return to it, words that are not precise, sentences that are not clear, and explanations that do not explain enough will be easier to spot."[19]

18. Arlov, *Wadsworth*, 107.
19 Ibid.

Writing Effective Course Assignments

In the two processes of editing and revising, you have to do the revising first in order to clarify ideas within paragraphs, chapters, and sub-chapters; then, do the editing on individual sentences changing words and phrases to make the sentence as concise as possible.[20] Hence, you should always remember that while revising deals with ideas in paragraphs, chapters and the whole essay, editing deals with the mechanics of sentences—the punctuations and typing errors within individual sentences.

After you have completed revising and editing your assignment, proofread it for the minor errors in spelling and punctuations before submitting for evaluation. Then, submit it confidently. Do not anticipate your assignment report to be perfect in order to submit it to your course lecturer for evaluation. Perfection is hardly achievable; however, it is something you should strive to it till the last minute! This is what all writers do with writing, especially writing argumentative essays like course assignments. Axelrod and Cooper have these words: "Most writers plan and revise their plans; they draft and revise their drafts; they write and read what they've written, then write some more. Even when they have a final draft, most writers reread it one more time—proofreading to edit for clarity, grammar and spelling."[21] Experienced authors warn you about the impossibility to achieve ultimate perfection when they say: "Perfection is a chimera—it can't be achieved and you can waste a lot of time and energy seeking the holy grail of the Perfect [assignment report]."[22] This statement indicates that writing a convincing and persuasive assignment is an endless struggle that culminates only when you have decided to submit it to the higher authorities for evaluation.

---

20. Brandon & Brandon, *Sentences, Paragraphs, and Beyond*, 289, cf. Mligo, *Introduction to Research Methods*, 128–130.
21 Axelrod & Cooper, *The St. Martin's Guide*, 8.
22 Epistein, Kenway & Boden, *Writing for Publication*, 55.

CONSTRUCTING AN INFORMED ARGUMENT

Chapter Review Questions

1. What is an argument? List the four (4) important points for a good argument.
2. The argument can either be *exploratory* or *persuasive*. What type of argument between the two is used in academic writing, and why?
3. State how the arguments of fact, of action, and of refutation are organized?
4. List the main components of an argument. Explain each component by providing an example of a simple argument of fact.
5. Discuss the features of a well-presented argument.
6. What is the difference between inductive and deductive structures of arguments? Using relevant examples illustrate how each structure works. Discuss the following concepts as used in deductive arguments: sound and unsound arguments, syllogism, valid and invalid syllogism, valid and true syllogism, valid but untrue syllogism, and enthymeme.
7. What is a fallacy in reasoning? What causes reasoning to be fallacious? Mention and discuss, with examples, the fallacies highlighted in this chapter. State how you can avoid bias when arguing your case.

Chapter 7

CONCLUSION

WRITING A SIMPLE BOOK to guide someone to grasp what is not clear to him or her has always been so difficult to most authors, including me. This difficulty arises because of several questions. The first question is "what": what is it that the student does not fully grasp and requires simplicity in order to grasp it? This is the question of appropriation of the needed materials to the author's intended audience. The second question is based on the needed level of simplicity: what level of simplicity is adequate to all students, in their diverse disciplines of specialty, to grasp what is required of them? This question is about diction—the level of depth the author should attempt to present materials in order to meet the needs of the audience.

Both questions above are pressing ones in writing a simple guidebook for students. In this case, this book does not promise to have exhausted the simplicity and diction requirements for all students reading the book as per questions raised above; rather, it promises all students to have covered most of what is required of them in their junior levels of university and college learning to write effective course assignments to fulfill their academic requirements.

The book has covered a wide range of important issues. It has presented the definition of an assignment and its relation to

CONCLUSION

research in general, how the student can move from an assignment question to topic for research, how the student can map the strategy for investigating the problem of the assignment through reviewing the various written materials, formulating the questions to address the problem, assembling the relevant materials to deal with the questions, and constructing tentative and complete theses as standpoints for the assignment which is followed by the actual research. More important is the writing stage using the obtained information. It is here that you will have to use sources in order to construct an informed argument for your assignment.

The book has further discussed the structure of an argument, its components, its features, the fallacies in argumentation, and how to avoid bias in arguing your case. However, the argument is incomplete without using other people's works. This book has provided a definition of what entails using sources. It has described the important citations (integral and non-integral citations) and how they work, the use of reporting verbs, and the role of citations in the writing process. It also discussed how omissions and additions of materials can be handled in the use of other people's words.

Moreover, the book has dealt with the question of documentation of sources you cite using the main established documentation styles, or your own creatively constructed documentation style. It also discussed how you can present your ideas systematically in terms of chapters and paragraphs to make the whole argument of the assignment both logical and convincing to your readers. The discussions of the issues of unity of the argument, supporting evidence and its credibility, coherence of argument ideas, emphasis of stated points through the repetition of words and sentence structures, has been provided in order to construct a smoothly flowing argument.

I sincerely hope that your proper use of this book will not only save the time and energy of lecturers to supervise your assignments, but also reduce unnecessary pressure for you to think about what you are supposed to do. This is because most of what is required for a strong and convincing course assignment has been honestly covered in this book.

BIBLIOGRAPHY

Aaron, Jane E. *The Little, Brown Essential Handbook*. Sixth Edition. New York, NY.: Longman, 2009.

———. *LB Brief: The Little Brown Handbook, Brief Version*. Second Edition. New York, NY.: Pearson Education, 2005.

———. *The Little, Brown Compact Handbook*. Third Edition. New York, NY.: Addison-Wesley, 1998.

Akoko, Robert Mbe. *"Ask and You will be Given": Pentecostalism and the Economic Crisis in Cameroon*. Leiden: African Studies, 2007.

Anker, Susan. *Real Essays with Readings: Writing Projects for College, Work and Everyday Life*. Boston, MA.: Bedford/St. Martin's, 2009.

———. *Real Essays with Readings: Writing Projects for College, Work and Everyday Life*. Boston, MA.: Bedford/St. Martin's, 2010.

Arlov, Pamela. *Wordsmith: A Guide to College Writing*. Fourth Edition. Upper Saddle River, NJ.: Prentice–Hall, 2010.

Axelrod, Rise B. and Cooper, Charles R. *The St.Martin's Guide to Writing*. Fourth Edition. New York, NY.: St. Martin's Press, 1994.

Baker, Sheridan. *The Practical Stylist*. Fourth Edition. New York, NY.: Thomas Y. Crowell Company, 1977.

Biggam, John. *Succeeding with Your Master's Dissertation: A Step-by-Step Handbook*. Second Edition. New York, NY.: McGraw Hill, 2011.

Blau, Sheridan, Elbow, Peter and Killgallon. *The Writer's Craft*. Evanston, Illinois: McDougal, Littel & Company, 1995.

Brandon, Lee and Brandon, Kelly. *Sentences, Paragraphs, and Beyond. With Integrated Readings*. Fifth Edition. Boston, MA.: Houghton Mifflin, 2008.

Bullock, Richard & Weinberg, Francine. *The Little Seagull Handbook*. New York, NY.: W.W. Norton & Company, 2011.

———. *The Norton Field Guide to Writing with a Handbook*. Second Edition. New York, NY.: W.W. Norton & Company, 2009.

Crusius, Tmothy W and Channell, Carolyn E. *The Aims of Argument: A Rhetoric and Reader*. Fourth Edition. Boston, MA.: McGraw-Hill Education, 2010.

BIBLIOGRAPHY

_____. *The Aims of Argument: A Rhetoric and Reader.* Mountain View, CA.: Mayfield, 1995.

Epistein, Debbie, Kenway, Jane and Boden, Rebecca. *Writing for Publication.* London: Sage, 2005.

Kirszner, Laurie G. and Mandell, Stephen R. *The Concise Wadsworth Handbook.* Toronto, Ontario: Thomson Wadsworth, 2005.

Hacker, Diana. *A Writer's Reference.* Fifth Edition. Boston, MA.: Bedford/St. Martin's, 2003.

Hacker, Diana and Somer, Nancy. *The Bedford Handbook.* Eighth Edition. Boston, MA.: Bedford/St. Martin's, 2010.

Hall, Donald. *Writing Well.* Sixth Edition. Glenview, Illinois: Scott, Foresman and Company, 1988.

Howard, Rebbeca Moore. *Writing Matters: A Handbook for Writing and Research.* New York, NY.: McGraw Hill, 2011.

Heineman, Alan and Willis, Hulon. *Writing Term Papers.* Third Edition. San Diego: Harcourt Brace Jovanovich, 1988.

Kafyulilo, Ayoub. "Access, Use and Perceptions of Teachers and Students towards Mobile Phones as a Tool for Teaching and Learning in Tanzania." *Education Information Technology,* 2012.

Kothari, C.R. *Research Methodology: Methods and Techniques.* Second Revised Edition. New Delhi: New Age International, 2004.

Kuhlthau, Carol Collier. *Teaching the Library Research Process: A Step-by-Step Programme for Secondary School Students.* West Nyack, NY.: The Centre for Applied Research in Education, 1985.

Lester, D. James & Lester James. *Writing Research Papers: A Complete Guide.* Tenth Edition. Addison-Wesley, 2002.

Lundford, Ronald and Bridges, Bill. *The Longwood Guide to Writing.* Brief Edition. Needham, MA.: Allyn & Bacon, 2000.

Mapugilo, Aidan W. *Communication and Study Skills for Undergraduates: A Manual.* Mbeya: Teofilo Kisanji University, 2007.

Markus, Mimi. *Write Time, Write Place: Paragraphs and Essays.* Annotated Instructor's Edition. Boston, MA.: Longman, 2011.

Mligo, Elia Shabani. *Introduction to Research Methods and Report Writing: A Practical Guide for Students and Researchers in Social Sciences and the Humanities.* Eugene, OR.: Wipf and Stock/Resource, 2016.

_____. *Doing Effective Fieldwork: A Textbook for Students of Qualitative Field Research in Higher-Learning Institutions.* Eugene, OR.: Wipf and Stock/Resource, 2013.

_____. *Writing Academic Papers: A Resource Manual for Beginners in Higher-Learning Institutions and Colleges.* Eugene, OR.: Wipf and Stock/Resource, 2012.

Monippally, Mathukutty M. and Pawar, Badrinarayan Shankar. *Academic Writing: A Guide to Management Students and Researchers.* New Delhi: Response Books, 2010.

BIBLIOGRAPHY

Mugyenyi, Apolo A. *Aspects of Sociology, Philosophy, Management, and Administration.* Moshi: Moshi Printing Press, 2013.

Nkoko, Baraka M. *Practical Communication Skills: A Reliable Reference for Universities and Colleges.* Dar es Salaam: Good Books, 2013.

Peccorari, Diane. *Academic Writing and Plagiarism.* New York, NY.: Continuum, 2008.

Raimes, Ann. *Pocket Keys for Writers.* Third Edition. Boston, MA.: Wadsworth, 2010.

_____. *Keys for Writers.* Fifth Edition. New York, NY.: Houghton Mifflin, 2008.

Seyler, Dorothy U. *Read, Reason, Write: An Argument Text and Reader.* New York, NY.: McGraw Hill, 2008.

Skwire, Sarah E. and Skwire, David. *Writing with a Thesis.* Ninth Edition. New York, NY.: Wadsworth, 2005.

Tibbetts, A. M. and Tibbetts, Charlene. *Strategies of Rhetoric.* Glenview, Illinois: Scott, Foresman and Company, 1979.

Trimble, John R. *Writing with Style: Conversations on the Art of Writing.* Second Edition. Upper Saddle River, NJ.: Prentice-Hall, 2000.

Vyhmeister, Jean Nancy. *Quality Research Papers: For Students of Religion and Theology.* Grand Rapids, Michigan: Zondervan, 2008.

Wiener, Harvey S. and Bezerman, Charles. *Basic Reading Skills Handbook.* Sixth Edition. New York, NY.: Pearson Education, 2006.

Williams, Joseph M. *Style: Toward Clarity and Grace.* Chicago and London: The University of Chicago Press, 1990.

William, Zinsser. *On Writing Well: An Informal Guide to Writing Nonfiction.* Third Edition-Revised and Enlarged. New York, NY.: Herper and Ro, 1985.

Yakhontova, T.V. *English Academic Writing for Students and Researchers,* 2003.

www.ingramcontent.com/pod-product-compliance
Lightning Source LLC
Chambersburg PA
CBHW071433160426
43195CB00013B/1877